Crochet
For Absolute Beginners

Your Step-by-Step Illustrated Guide with Basic Stitches and Easy Handmade Crochet Projects

Alexandra Davis

© Copyright 2024 Alexandra Davis
All Rights Reserved.
Protected with www.protectmywork.com,
Reference Number: 17230031124S083

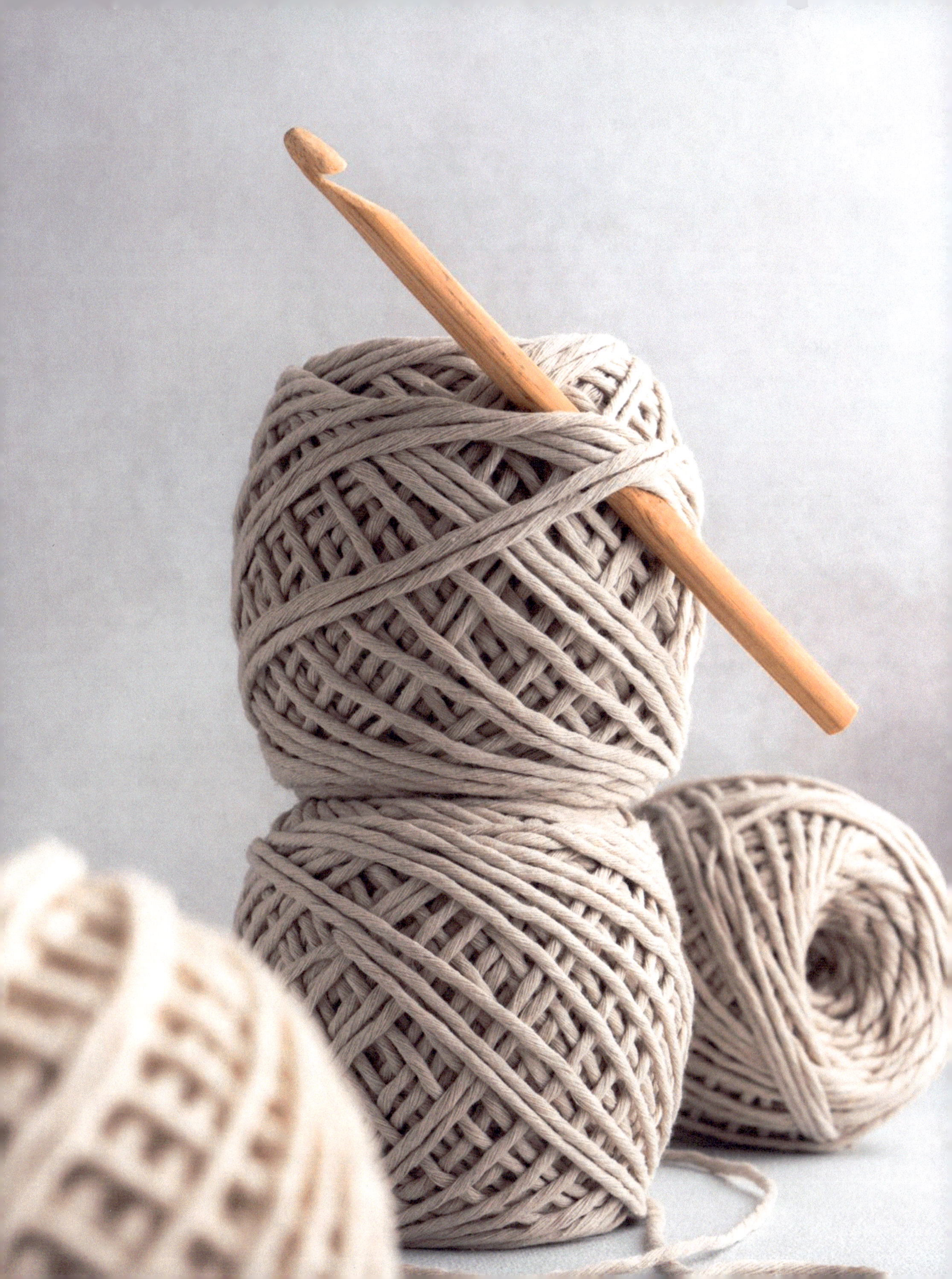

TABLE OF CONTENTS

INTRODUCTION

CHAPTER 1: TOOLS AND MATERIALS

HOOKS 8
YARN 12
OTHER TOOLS 16
COMMON ABBREVIATIONS 17

CHAPTER 2: READING CROCHET SYMBOLS, PATTERNS, AND DIAGRAMS

CROCHET SYMBOLS 18
CROCHET PATTERNS 19
UNDERSTANDING DIAGRAMS/CHARTS 21

CHAPTER 3: BASIC TECHNIQUES

WORKING END AND TAIL END 23
YARN OVER 24
SLIP KNOT 25
CHAIN STITCH (CH) 27
FOUNDATION CHAIN 28
TURNING CHAIN (TCH) 29
CHAIN CIRCLE 29
MAGIC RING 30
PARTS OF THE STITCH 30
HOW TO COUNT STITCHES 31
TIPS FOR MAINTAINING AN EVEN TENSION ... 31

CHAPTER 4: BASIC STITCHES

SLIP STITCH (SL ST) 32
SINGLE CROCHET (SC) 33
EXTENDED SINGLE CROCHET (ESC) 34
HALF DOUBLE CROCHET (HDC) 35
DOUBLE CROCHET (DC) 36
TREBLE CROCHET (TR) 37
DOUBLE TREBLE CROCHET (DTR) 38
REVERSE SINGLE CROCHET 39
HOW TO CHANGE COLOR AND WORK IN STRIPES 39
METHODS OF INCREASE AND DECREASE 40

4 BASIC STITCHES TO TRY

BASIC SINGLE CROCHET PATTERN SQUARE ... 41
BASIC DOUBLE CROCHET PATTERN 43
BASIC HALF DOUBLE CROCHET PATTERN 44
BASIC TREBLE CROCHET PATTERN 45

CHAPTER 5: CIRCULAR CROCHET

SIMPLE CIRCULAR COASTER 46
TROUBLESHOOTING CIRCULAR CROCHET 48

CHAPTER 6: SPECIAL STITCHES

- SINGLE CROCHET RIB STITCH 49
- MESH 50
- POST STITCHES 50
- V-STITCH 51
- SHELL STITCH 51
- PUFF STITCH 52
- POPCORN STITCH 52
- PICOT STITCH 53

CHAPTER 7: GRANNY SQUARES

- BASIC GRANNY SQUARE WITH COLOR CHANGES 54
- SOLID GRANNY SQUARE 56
- GRANNY SQUARE WITH A CIRCULAR CENTER . 56
- HEXAGON GRANNY SQUARE 57
- TRIANGLE GRANNY SQUARE 57
- GRANNY SQUARE COASTERS 58
- GRANNY SQUARE BLANKET 59

CHAPTER 8: EASY PROJECTS FOR BEGINNERS

- SIMPLE DISHCLOTH 61
- EAR WARMER 62
- BASIC BEANIE 63
- SHAWL 65
- SCARF 66
- BLANKET 68
- PILLOW 70
- BAG 72
- GLOVES 74
- SIMPLE CARDIGAN 76

EASY CHRISTMAS PROJECTS

- CHRISTMAS TREE ORNAMENT 78
- CHRISTMAS STOCKING 79
- CHRISTMAS WREATH 80

CHAPTER 9: COMMON CROCHET PROBLEMS AND SOLUTIONS

APPENDIX

- GLOSSARY OF CROCHET TERMS AND ABBREVIATIONS 84

BONUS

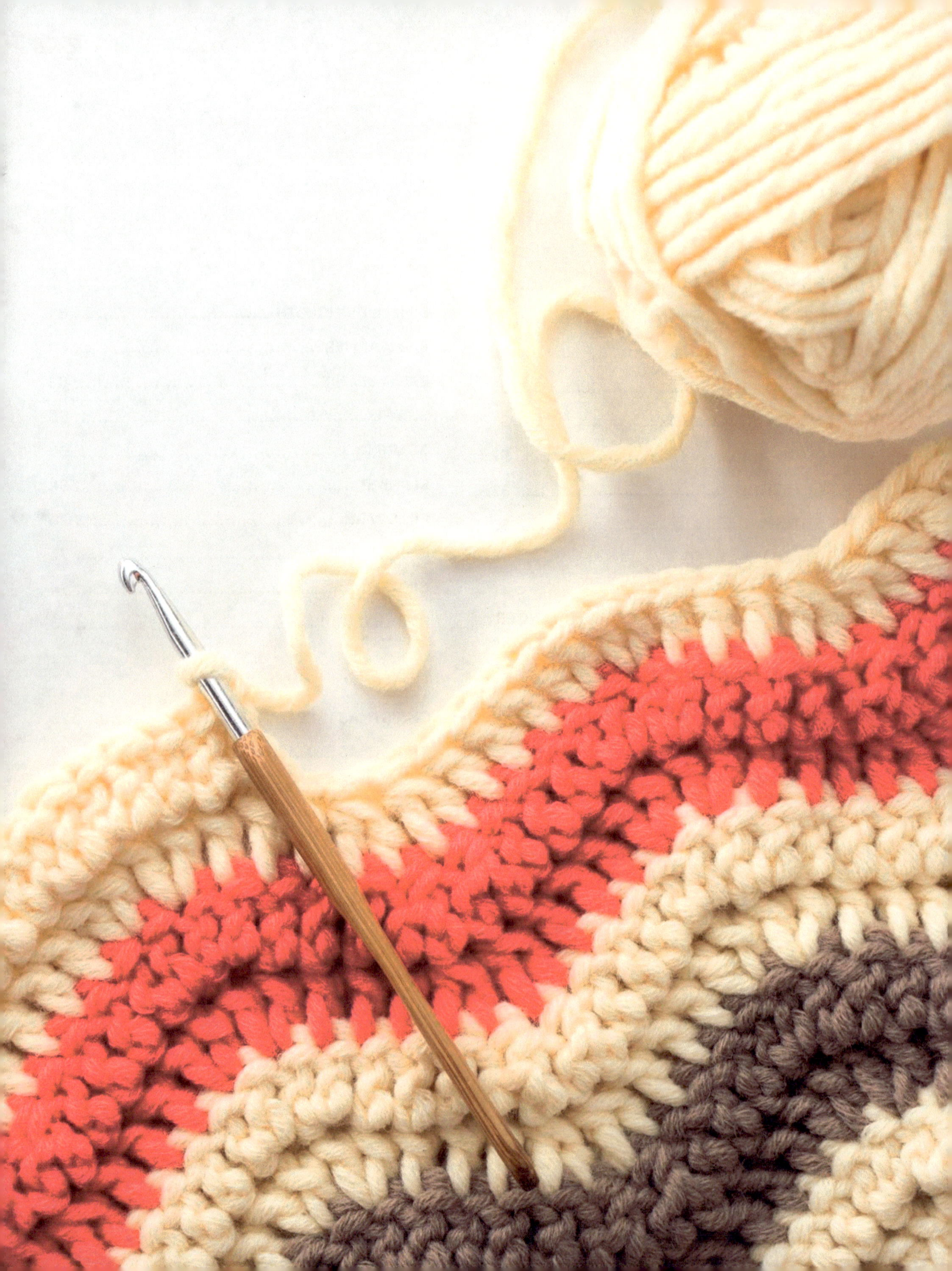

INTRODUCTION

Welcome to the fascinating world of crochet, a universe where creativity, relaxation, and art are intertwined in every bow and every stitch. If you're reading these lines, you're probably looking for a way to disconnect from the daily routine, find a calm space in your busy life, and, why not, explore a new facet of your creativity.

For centuries, this technique has been a means of creating both practical and charming objects. From cozy blankets to delicate decorations, it offers a wide range of possibilities that enrich our environment and our lives.

But crochet is more than a hobby; it is an activity that promotes calm, concentration, and emotional well-being. In the rhythmic sequence of the stitches, you will find a space of tranquility and reflection, a form of active meditation that will allow you to reconnect with yourself and break away from daily stress.

In this book, I'll take you by the hand through the fundamentals of its foundations. It doesn't matter if you've never held a hook in your life; the following pages are designed to guide you from the most basic concepts to the completion of charming and practical projects. Together, we'll discover how to master your first stitch, and undertake simple yet rewarding works that will adorn your home and can become gifts for your loved ones. This book results from years of practice, teaching, and, above all, an unwavering passion. Here you will find clear instructions and useful tips to make each step as pleasant as it is enriching.

The first chapter is designed to lay the foundation; we will address the fundamental aspects of this art, from choosing the right yarn and hook to understanding the basic terms. This chapter is so that, as a beginner, you feel comfortable and confident when taking your first steps. The second chapter will equip you to interpret patterns and symbols. This ability will open up a world of possibilities for you, allowing you to follow instructions to create many beautiful pieces.

In the third and fourth chapters, I'll walk you through creating your first basic stitches. Here, practice and patience will be your best allies. Don't worry about perfection. Remember, every stitch is a step forward in your learning journey.

The fifth chapter will introduce you to the circular technique. This approach will allow you to create pieces with unique shapes and is ideal for hats, amigurumi (crochet dolls), and home decorations. The sixth chapter is intended for those who, having mastered the fundamentals, wish to take their art further. We will explore more complex techniques, opening the door to a wider world of creative possibilities.

In the seventh and eighth chapters, you will find a selection of works designed for beginners. These will be a fun and rewarding way to apply your newly learned skills; they will give you the satisfaction of seeing your efforts materialize in beautiful creations. From colorful Granny Squares to elegant scarves, each has been selected with simplicity and beauty in mind. In the chapter nine, you will find answers to the most frequently asked questions and problems that may arise throughout your training.

In addition to these chapters, the book includes an appendix with a glossary of terms and abbreviations, an invaluable tool for any weaver.

This book is designed with the absolute beginner in mind, ensuring that anyone, regardless of their background or experience, can pick up a hook and start crocheting. I've tailored the content to be as inclusive and accessible as possible, breaking down complex ideas into straightforward, manageable steps. My goal is to provide you with the technical knowledge, inspiration, and support for your success in this exciting world. My greatest desire is to share the warmth and satisfaction it has brought to my life, which has taught me that every stitch is an expression of creativity, every job completed is a celebration of patience and effort, and each piece created is a treasure trove of memories and love.

So, gather your yarn and hook, find a cozy spot, and let's embark on this creative journey together.

WELCOME TO THE WORLD OF CROCHET!

CHAPTER 1
TOOLS AND MATERIALS

This first chapter is essential; you will discover the basic elements, from selecting the right hook and yarn to familiarizing yourself with the tools to make your experience smooth and pleasant. Understanding these fundamentals is crucial to making your future projects successful and rewarding.

Tackling the basics may seem simple, but in reality, it is where the heart of every great work lies. By learning about the different types of hooks and yarns; and how to choose them, you'll be building a solid foundation for your skills.

Here are the different types of materials and tools you should gather:

HOOKS

A hook is a fundamental tool in crochet, consisting of a slender handle with a hook at one end. This hook pulls yarn or thread through loops to create stitches. Although it seems simple at first glance, each part of the hook has a specific function to ease and efficiency.

- **Head**: The most important part. Its shape allows the yarn to slide and hold during the process; it varies in size and shape, which is critical in determining the size.
- **Throat**: It is the inclined part that leads to the axis. The throat helps guide the yarn from the head to the shaft to maintain the correct yarn tension.
- **Grip**: Located in the center, this is where the grip is held. It can have an ergonomic design for comfort during prolonged crocheting.
- **Handle**: The end, which provides balance and support while crocheting, could be longer and more ergonomic, more so in those designed to minimize hand fatigue.

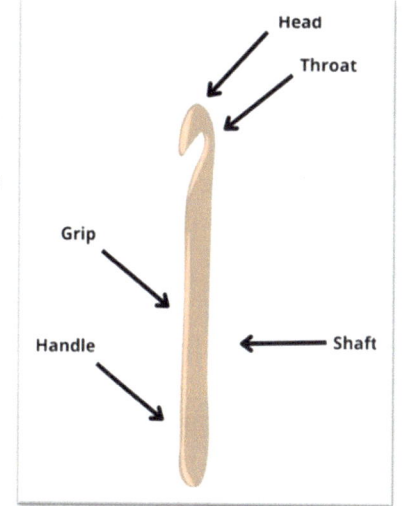

DIFFERENT TYPES OF HOOKS

There are several types of crochet hooks, each with unique properties suitable for different types of yarns, techniques, and personal preferences. The choice makes a big difference in the ease, comfort of the hands, and the quality of the final work.

Types of hooks:

- **Aluminum**: They are the most common and versatile. Lightweight and with a smooth surface, they facilitate the sliding of the yarn. They are ideal for beginners and work well with most yarns.
- **Steel**: Smaller and thinner, they are used for fine yarns and delicate work such as lace. Their small size makes them perfect for detailed fabrics.
- **Plastic**: Lightweight and economical, they are a good choice for thick yarns and large projects. They are comfortable to hold and are usually larger than aluminum or steel ones.
- **Bamboo and Wood**: They are appreciated for their warmth and natural texture. They are soft, light, and comfortable, ideal for those who have joint problems or prefer a more organic feel. They work well with yarns that can be snagged on metal hooks.
- **Ergonomic**: Designed to minimize stress on the hands and wrists, these have larger handles and are often molded to fit in the hand. They are ideal for those who spend many hours crocheting or for those who have arthritis or pain in their hands.
- **Adjustable or Interchangeable**: These allow you to change the shaft size, making them versatile. They are useful for those who enjoy a variety of styles and patterns.
- **Tunisian or Afghan**: They are longer than traditional ones and are used for a specific technique known as Tunisian.
- **Lighted**: Ideal for working with dark yarns or in low-light conditions, these have a built-in LED light that illuminates the work area.

Choosing the right crochet hook depends on the yarn you plan to use. Each yarn label recommends a hook size to achieve a standard gauge. For beginners, a medium-size hook (H/8 or 5mm) is ideal as it's comfortable to hold and works well with medium-weight yarns.

Experimenting with different types of hooks is an exciting and enriching part of your journey, allowing you to discover which tools best suit your personal technique and needs.

In the end, choosing the right one comes down to personal preference, as each weaver has their own unique style and specific requirements.

Here's a table showing the correspondence between hook sizes in metric (mm) and the system used in the United States. Please note that some sizes vary between different manufacturers.

METRIC SIZE (MM)	SIZE US
2.25	B-1
2.75	C-2
3.25	D-3
3.50	E-4
3.75	F-5
4.00	G-6
4.50	7
5.00	H-8
5.50	I-9
6.00	J-10
6.50	K-10.5
8.00	L-11
9.00	M-13
10.00	N-15
12.00	P-16

HOW TO HOLD THE HOOK

Holding the hook correctly is necessary to crochet efficiently and comfortably. It can be done in two ways: the pencil grip or the knife grip.

In the pencil grip, hold the hook like a pencil, with the handle resting in your palm and your thumb and index finger grasping it. This method of holding is one of the most popular and effective for beginners. It allows good control over the hook and yarn, facilitating the creation of uniform stitches and efficient handling.

The knife grip involves holding the hook like you would a knife, with the handle resting on the palm of your hand and the fingers wrapped around it. This grip is comfortable for longer periods of crocheting and allows for quicker stitching.

Experiment with both grips to find which feels more natural. Remember, the key to successful crocheting is comfort and consistency in your tension. As you practice, you'll find the grip that best suits your style, helping you create even stitches and beautiful projects.

YARN

Just as a painter chooses her colors and textures, a weaver selects her yarn with care and consideration, knowing that this will be the basis of her work.

It comes in an amazing variety of types, each with unique characteristics. From soft and breathable cotton, ideal for summer garments and household items, to warm and cozy wools, perfect for blankets and winter garments. Acrylic yarns offer a vibrant color palette and are a durable and easy-care option; while, blends of natural and synthetic fibers combine the best of both worlds, offering both functionality and beauty.

The choice of yarn influences the texture and final appearance of the piece. Thicker yarns create robust fabrics, ideal for quick jobs or those just starting. Finer yarns, on the other hand, allow for exquisite detail and are perfect for delicate and complex work. The weight and thickness of the yarn determine the appearance, the size to wear, and the pattern.

DIFFERENT TYPES OF YARN AND THEIR WEIGHTS

There is a wide variety of yarns available, each with its own peculiarities and recommended uses. Understanding the different types of yarn and their weights helps you choose the right material:

Cotton

- A versatile and durable yarn, ideal for summer garments, kitchen accessories, and baby projects. It is known for its absorbency and ease of care.
- Weight: Available in a wide range, from Light to Medium (Worsted) and Heavy (Bulky).

Wool

- It is a natural and warm yarn, perfect for winter garments and accessories. The wool is stretchy, making it ideal for garments that require comfort and fit.
- Weight: Varies from Lace and Light to Medium (Worsted, Aran) and Heavy (Bulky, Super Bulky).

Acrylic

- Synthetic fiber is popular for its durability, variety of colors, and ease of care. It is an economical and resistant option.
- Weight: Available in all weights, from Fine to Super Bulky.

Fiber Blends

- They combine the qualities of different fibers, such as wool and acrylic, to balance softness, durability, and ease of care.
- Weight: Varies depending on the blend, offering a wide range from Fine to Bulky.

Silk

- It is a luxurious, soft yarn with a natural shine. It is ideal for elegant garments and accessories.
- Weight: Available in lighter weights such as Lace and Super Fine.

Bamboo

- A soft and silky yarn with antibacterial and absorption properties that is cool and comfortable, ideal for summer clothes and accessories.
- Weight: In light weights, giving a fluid fall and softness to the touch.

Cashmere

- It is a soft and luxurious yarn, known for its warmth and lightness, and ideal for high-end accessories and garments.
- Weight: Found in lightweights such as Fine.

Mohair

- Coming from the wool of the Angora goat, mohair is known for its luster and ethereal texture. It is often combined with other yarns to add volume and warmth.
- Weight: It varies from light (Lace) to thicker weights (Bulky) used with other yarns.

Chenille

- It is a soft, velvety yarn known for its unique texture and luxurious look. It is popular for blankets and decorative accessories.
- Weight: Available In medium weights such as Worsted and Aran.

The yarn label is your guide, providing weight, recommended hook size, and care instructions. For beginners, medium-weight yarn (worsted) is a versatile choice, easy to handle and suitable for a wide range of projects.

Here's a table that presents the different weights of crochet yarn, categorized from Fine/Lace to Jumbo, with their equivalents in weight units according to the system known in the U.S. (ounces per yard):

WEIGHT	HOOK SIZE	COMMON USES
Lace (0)	Steel 6,7,8, Regular, B-1 (1.40mm-2.25mm)	Lace, Doilies, Fine Amigurumi
Super Fine (1)	B-1 to E-4 (2.25mm-3.5mm)	Socks, Baby Items, Lace
Fine (2)	E-4 to 7 (3mm-4mm)	Light Garments, Baby Items, Accessories
Light (3)	7 to I-9 (3.5mm-5mm)	Sweaters, Garments, Lightweight, Scarves
Medium (4)	I-9 to K-10.5 (4mm-6mm)	Sweaters, Blankets, Hats, Scarves, Mittens
Bulky (5)	K-10.5 to M-13 (5.5mm-9mm)	Rugs, Jackets, Blankets
Super Bulky (6)	M-13 to Q (9mm-15mm)	Heavy Blankets, Rugs, Home Decor
Jumbo (7)	Q + (15mm+)	Home Decor

YARN CHOICE BASED ON PROJECT TYPE

Clothes

When making garments, comfort and adaptability are crucial. For items that will be in direct contact with the skin, such as sweaters, socks, or hats, it is recommended to choose soft and breathable yarns. Cotton and cotton blends are excellent for summer clothing, while wool and its blends are ideal for winter garments due to their insulating properties. For luxury or specialty garments, consider silk or cashmere.

For Babies

Baby items require soft, hypoallergenic, and easy-to-wash yarns. Cotton and acrylic are popular for their softness and durability. Avoid yarns that can cause irritation or have small parts that can come off, such as buttons or sequins.

Household Items

For items like blankets, cushions, or rugs, look for strong, durable yarns. Acrylic and synthetic blends are robust options, as they hold up well to frequent use and regular washing. For a more luxurious décor, consider heavier yarns or unique textures.

Amigurumis and Toys

Amigurumis require yarns that hold their shape well and allow for precise details. Mercerized cotton or acrylic are excellent options for their firmness and variety of colors because the yarn is resistant and does not fray.

Accessories and Details

For accessories such as scarves, shawls, or bags, choose yarns that complement the item's function, for example, for a warm scarf, opt for wool or alpaca; for a lightweight shawl, choose silk or a fine yarn.

When choosing yarn, then consider the project's purpose but also the care that the finished item will require. Some yarns need special care, such as hand washing or dry cleaning, while others are machine washed and dried.

Remember, the joy of crochet comes from creating something unique. Feel free to experiment with different yarns, observing how they work up and how they feel in your hands. This exploration will not only enhance your skills but also expand your creative possibilities, making each project a personal expression of your craft.

In the end, the best guide is your experience and preferences, along with the specific needs you have in mind.

OTHER TOOLS

Each of these tools serves a specific purpose and enhances the creation process:

- **Scissors:** Good scissors should be small and sharp, ideal for cutting yarns accurately. It is an indispensable tool for finishing a job or changing yarn color.

- **Open or split-ring stitch markers**: They are indispensable for marking the beginning of a round or noting where increases or decreases occur. These markers can easily be clipped onto your work and removed without damaging the yarn. For beginners, brightly colored markers can be especially helpful for easy visibility against your work. They make the count easier, preventing errors.

- **Tapestry needles**: Also known as yarn needles, have a large eye suitable for threading yarn. These needles are used to weave in ends of yarn at the completion of a project or to sew pieces together. Opt for a set with different sizes to fit different yarn weights.

- **Swatch ruler and needle/hook gauge**: They serve dual purposes. The swatch ruler helps you measure your work accurately, ensuring that your project dimensions are correct. The needle/hook gauge is a tool with holes of various sizes to measure your hook or needle size. This is particularly useful if the size marking on your hook or needle has worn off.

- **T-pins**: Used in blocking, the process of shaping and setting your finished project to its final dimensions. T-pins are pushed into a blocking mat to hold your work in place. Choose stainless steel pins to avoid rust.

- **Blocking mat**: It provides a flat surface for your projects to dry in the desired shape. Look for mats that are grid-lined to assist in aligning your work precisely.

- **Gentle no-rinse cleaner**: It is recommended for washing your projects. These cleansers are designed to be delicate on fibers, ensuring your handcrafted items remain soft and vibrant without the need for harsh rinsing.

- **Tape measure**: To measure dimensions.

- **Notebook and pencil**: To write patterns, make adjustments, or draw diagrams. A journal is an invaluable resource for tracking your progress.

- **Pattern book or online pattern access**: A source of inspiration and guidance. Patterns give you detailed instructions and help you learn new techniques.

- **Bag or case**: Keep your hooks, scissors, and other small accessories organized and protected. A bag is ideal for carrying your projects with you.

Each of these tools plays a specific role in the creation and finishing of crochet projects, making them essential additions to your toolkit. Selecting quality tools that suit your needs will enhance your crocheting experience, leading to beautifully finished projects.

COMMON ABBREVIATIONS

ABBREVIATION	MEANING USA
ch	Chain
YO	Yarn Over
st	Stitch
sl st	Slip Stitch
sc	Single Crochet
dc	Double Crochet
tr	Treble Crochet
hdc	Half Double Crochet
dec	Decreasing Stitches
inc	Increasing Stitches
pc	Popcorns
sc2tog	Single Crochet Decrease
dc2tog	Double Crochet Decrease
rnd (s)	Round (s)

Here's a table comparing common abbreviations used in the United States and the United Kingdom, along with their meanings. This table is useful, as the same abbreviations have different meanings in these two systems:

US TERMS	UK TERMS
Chain **(ch)**	Chain **(ch)**
Slip Stitch **(sl st)**	Slip Stitch **(ss)**
Single Crochet **(sc)**	Double Crochet **(dc)**
Double Crochet **(dc)**	Treble Crochet **(tc)**
Half Double Crochet **(hdc)**	Half Treble Crochet **(htc)**

CHAPTER 2
READING CROCHET SYMBOLS, PATTERNS, AND DIAGRAMS

CROCHET SYMBOLS

Here are the common symbols and their corresponding stitches:

SYMBOL	NAME
○ OR ⬭	Chain (ch)
●	Slip Stitch (sl st)
+ OR X	Single Crochet (sc)
T	Half Double Crochet (hdc)
╪	Double Crochet (dc)
╪	Treble Crochet (tr)
╪	Double Treble Crochet (dtr)
⋀	Single Crochet Decrease (sc2tog)
⋀	Double Crochet Decrease (dc2tog)
◯	Magic Ring (mr)

Each symbol represents a specific technique or stitch, and its mastery is essential for any weaver.

Keep in mind the following tips:

- Familiarize yourself with the symbols by practicing with small samples. This will help you understand how each symbol translates into a specific stitch.

- Use books, videos, and online resources to see how these techniques are performed.

- Having a glossary or symbol legend on hand is an invaluable tool when working with patterns from different sources.

CROCHET PATTERNS

When you first encounter a crochet pattern, the array of abbreviations and symbols might seem like a foreign language. However, with a bit of guidance, you'll soon learn to decode these instructions and embark on creating beautiful crochet pieces. Written patterns provide a roadmap for your project, detailing every stitch and turn your hook must make.

UNDERSTANDING WRITTEN PATTERNS

Here's how to navigate these patterns with confidence.

Start by looking at the pattern's introduction, which often includes the project's size, the recommended yarn type, hook size, gauge (the number of stitches per inch), and a list of abbreviations used. Understanding the gauge is crucial; it ensures that your project matches the intended size and that you have enough yarn to complete it.

Next, patterns typically begin with a foundation chain instruction, indicating how many chains to make. For example, "Ch 50" means you'll make 50 chain stitches. This foundation chain serves as the base for your project.

The body of the pattern follows, broken down into rows or rounds. Each row or round will start with a stitch count, such as "Row 1: Sc in 2nd ch from hook and in each ch across (49 sc)." This tells you to make a single crochet (sc) in the second chain from your hook and in each chain across the row, resulting in 49 single crochets.

Patterns may include repeats. An asterisk (*) is used to indicate the beginning of a series of stitches within a given row, followed by instructions like "repeat from * to ". This means you'll repeat the sequence of stitches between the asterisks the specified number of times.

To finish, patterns often provide finishing instructions, such as how to fasten off your yarn and weave in ends. They may also include assembly instructions if the project consists of multiple pieces.

Remember, practice makes perfect. Start with simple patterns to build your confidence. Keep a list of common abbreviations by your side as a quick reference. With patience and practice, reading crochet patterns will become as natural as reading your favorite book.

Increases, Decreases, and Other Techniques

Patterns often include techniques such as increments (increasing the number) and decreases (reducing the number) to shape the tissue. These are necessary when a specific shape is required, such as hats, gloves, or amigurumis. The patterns include instructions for advanced techniques or special stitches that add texture and complexity.

Example Instruction: "Inc in the next stitch, sc in the next 2 stitches." You should increase (inc) by making two stitches in the same place, followed by a single crochet in the next two.

Color and Design Changes

Many patterns include color changes or instructions for following a graphic design. These changes are important for those that include multiple colors or complex patterns. The instructions will detail when and how to change the colors to achieve the desired design.

Example Instruction: "Change to color B at the end of row 5." Here, you are instructed to switch to the B color thread after completing row 5.

TIPS FOR FOLLOWING PATTERNS

Here is a list of brief but decisive tips:

1. **Start by Familiarizing Yourself with Abbreviations and Symbols**: Most crochet patterns use standardized abbreviations and symbols for stitches and techniques. For example, "ch" stands for chain stitch, "sc" for single crochet, and "dc" for double crochet. Before beginning, ensure you understand these abbreviations.

2. **Read Through the Entire Pattern First**: Before you start crocheting, read through the entire pattern. This overview gives you a sense of the project's scope, including any special techniques or stitch patterns you'll need to know. It's like reading a recipe before cooking; knowing what's ahead can prevent surprises.

3. **Gather Your Materials**: Patterns list the materials needed at the beginning. This includes the type and amount of yarn, the size of the crochet hook, and any additional tools or accessories. Using the recommended materials helps ensure your project turns out as intended. Substitutions can be made, but they may affect the size and appearance of the finished piece.

4. **Check the Gauge**: The gauge specifies how many stitches and rows per inch you should have using the recommended hook and yarn. It's crucial for projects where size matters, like garments. Make a test swatch to check your gauge. If your gauge is off, adjust by changing your hook size: a larger hook if your gauge is too tight, a smaller hook if it's too loose.

5. **Understand the Instructions**: Crochet patterns are typically written in a step-by-step format, often with a repeatable sequence of stitches. An asterisk (*) is used to indicate the beginning of a series of stitches within a given row, followed by instructions like "repeat from * to " which mean you repeat the sequence of stitches between the asterisks. Parentheses and brackets further group stitches or instructions that are worked together or repeated.

6. **Follow the Pattern Step-by-Step**: Begin your project by following the instructions line by line. Take your time, especially with new or complex stitches. It's not uncommon to need to read a line several times to fully understand it. If you make a mistake, simply unravel your work to the point of the error and try again.

7. **Mark Your Progress**: Use stitch markers or a row counter to keep track of your place in the pattern, especially if it involves repeating sequences or working in rounds. This can be particularly helpful if you need to put your project down and come back to it later.

8. **Finishing Touches**: Once you've completed the crocheting part, follow any finishing instructions in the pattern. This may include weaving in ends, blocking (shaping and setting your piece by wetting it, pinning it in place, and letting it dry), or assembling pieces.

9. **Practice and Patience**: Like any new skill, reading and following crochet patterns takes practice. Start with simpler projects to build your confidence and understanding. With patience and practice, you'll find your ability to interpret and execute patterns improves significantly.

UNDERSTANDING DIAGRAMS/CHARTS

Crochet diagrams or charts are visual representations of crochet patterns and are a universal language that can help you understand how to create a pattern regardless of the language in which the written instructions are provided. These diagrams use symbols to represent different stitches and are arranged to show the sequence and number of stitches needed.

Here's how to do it:

1. **Identify the Symbols:** Before you begin, familiarize yourself with the symbols used in the diagram. Each symbol corresponds to a specific type of stitch or technique. Most patterns include a legend or glossary that explains the meaning of each symbol.

2. **Understand the Starting Point and Direction:** Most crochet diagrams are read from the bottom up. Rows are typically read from right to left if you're right-handed, and left to right if you're left-handed. For circular patterns, you'll start in the center and work your way outwards in a spiral or round pattern.

3. **Locate the Beginning of the Diagram**, which could be a foundation chain or a magic ring.

4. **Follow the First Symbols in the Diagram**, which represent those of a chain (ch) or a slip knot. These will form the base, you must count on and follow the correct direction according to the diagram.

5. **Move Through the Diagram Following the Symbols One By One.** Each symbol will tell you which one you should do in that specific part. For example, a symbol in the shape of a "**+**" or "**x**" would indicate a single crochet (sc).

6. **Follow the Path of the Yarn:** The lines or arrows in the diagram show the path your yarn will take. In circular diagrams, you'll often see arrows guiding you on how to move from one round to the next. This helps in understanding not just the stitch, but also the direction in which to work.

7. **Count the Stitches:** Keep an accurate count of the stitches and rows so that they follow the size and shape indicated in the diagram. Use markers if necessary to mark the start of rounds or important stitches.

8. **Look for Repetition:** Some diagrams include repeats of a specific pattern within a row or round, marked with curly braces or asterisks, repeating the sequence the number of times indicated.

9. **Adjust Tension as Needed:** As you work, you may find that your tension affects the shape and size of your project. If your fabric is too tight or too loose compared to the diagram, adjust your grip on the yarn or hook size accordingly. Consistent tension is key to making your project look like the diagram.

10. **Use Stitch Markers for Complex Patterns:** For diagrams with intricate stitch placements or for circular patterns, use stitch markers to mark the beginning of rounds or specific stitches. This can help you keep your place and make it easier to follow the diagram accurately.

11. **Practice with a Simple Diagram:** Before tackling complex patterns, start with a basic diagram to familiarize yourself with reading and following the symbols. A simple square coaster or a granny square can be perfect for practice. You'll need medium-weight yarn (worsted), a size H/8 (5mm) crochet hook, and scissors. Begin by chaining the number of stitches indicated at the bottom of the diagram, then follow the symbols row by row or round by round, according to the diagram's progression.

CONTINUED →

12. **Diagrams Incorporate Color Changes or Special Techniques.** For example, a color change is marked with a different color symbol.

13. **More Complex Diagrams Include Advanced Ones such as the Puff or Popcorn.** Study how these are represented in the diagram and practice doing them before incorporating them. These usually have a distinctive symbol and require a combination of basic techniques.

14. **Compare Your Work to the Diagram to Know You're Following the Pattern.** This regular review will help you identify and fix bugs before you go too far.

15. **Continue to Follow the Diagram Row by Row or Round by Round,** it is vital to maintain the correct orientation of the diagram and see that you are moving in the right direction in each round.

16. **As You Go, Pay Special Attention to the Details of the Diagram,** such as the stitches where the rows meet, the corners in square or rectangular projects, and the increases or decreases in circular projects. These details are required to maintain the shape and design.

17. **Some Diagrams Include Smooth Transitions from One Technique to Another or Changes in Direction.** These changes are marked with specific symbols or marginal notes on the diagram.

18. For more advanced techniques, such as working around the posts of previous stitches or creating specific textures, study the representation of these in the diagram. It is helpful to practice these techniques separately before integrating them.

19. As you get closer to the end of the diagram, follow the symbols to the last one. This includes instructions for finishing, joining parts, or creating edges and finishes.

20. Once completed, compare it to the diagram so that everything matches. Check the shape, size, texture, and any specific details of the design.

CHAPTER 3
BASIC TECHNIQUES

WORKING END AND TAIL END

When you begin to crochet, you'll encounter two terms that are fundamental to understanding how to manage your yarn: the working end and the tail end.

The working end is the part of the yarn that is still connected to the ball or skein and is the one you will crochet with. As you crochet, the working end moves and becomes shorter, requiring you to occasionally pull more yarn from the yarn ball to continue.

On the other hand, the tail end is the loose end of the yarn. When you start a project, you'll make a slip knot on your hook, and the short piece of yarn that does not extend back to the yarn ball is the tail end. This end is not used in forming the stitches but is important for finishing your work neatly. After completing your project, you'll weave this tail end into your work with a tapestry needle to secure it and prevent unraveling

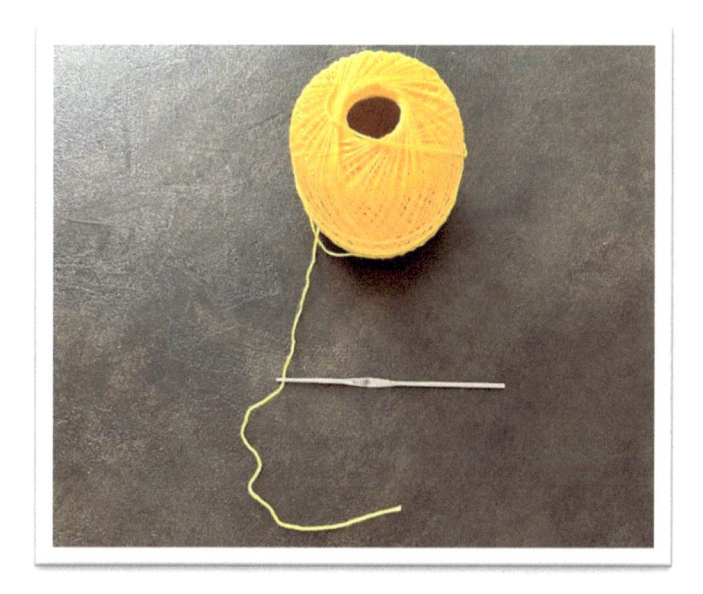

When you start crocheting, you should identify these extremes. A common mistake for beginners is to start crocheting with the tail end, which leads to undoing the work.

Managing these two ends is crucial for a tidy and successful crochet project. As you work, ensure the working end has enough slack to easily form stitches without tugging on the yarn ball. Keeping a moderate tension on the working end helps maintain even stitch sizes throughout your project. For the tail end, it's helpful to leave a length of about 6 inches when you start. This length makes it easier to weave in the end securely at the completion of your project.

Although these ends are not represented by specific symbols in diagrams, you must recognize and handle them for a clean and tidy beginning and end.

YARN OVER

Yarn over is a fundamental crochet technique used to create stitches, increase the size of a piece, or add decorative elements. It involves wrapping the yarn over the crochet hook to form a new loop. This action is crucial for making stitches such as the chain stitch, single crochet, and more complex stitches.

Here's how to execute a yarn over step by step:

1. Hold the Crochet Hook and Yarn Properly: Grip the hook with your dominant hand using either the pencil or knife hold. With your other hand, tension the yarn comfortably across your fingers to control the flow of yarn.

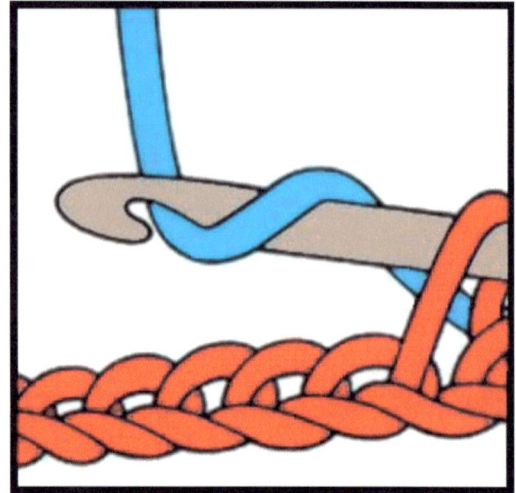

2. Position the Yarn and Hook: Ensure the working yarn (the yarn leading back to the skein) is behind the hook. The yarn should not be too tight or too loose to allow for smooth movement.

3. Execute the Yarn Over: Move the hook under and then over the working yarn. The motion is somewhat similar to turning a key in a lock. The hook should catch the yarn as it moves over it, creating a loop on the hook.

4. Complete the Stitch: Depending on the stitch you are working on, you will now pull this new loop through a loop already on the hook (for a single crochet) or through multiple loops (for more complex stitches).

5. Practice Consistency: The key to a neat crochet fabric is consistent tension in your yarn overs. Practice maintaining even pressure on the yarn and uniform loop sizes.

6. Repeat as Needed: Most crochet stitches require multiple yarn overs. Continue practicing this motion until it feels natural and you can perform it without looking.

Remember, mastering the yarn over is all about practice. It lays the foundation for almost every crochet stitch and is a technique you will use in every crochet project. As you become more comfortable with yarn overs, you will find your crochet work becoming faster and more even.

SLIP KNOT

The slip knot is the starting point from which you create the initial chains that form the basis of your work. Unlike other knots, the slip knot is unique because it can be easily adjusted and tightened or loosened with a simple pull, making it an essential skill for beginners to master.

The ability to tie a slip knot is important because it sets the tension and size of your chains and subsequent stitches. A well-made knot gets your work off to a smooth and smooth start.

When the working yarn is pulled, the knot closes around, holding it in place. The yarn tension is adjusted by pulling the free end of the yarn or loop, allowing it to move easily through the knot without slipping or loosening.

To form a slip knot, make a circle with the yarn, then thread under the circle and grab the yarn with the hook. When the working end is pulled, the yarn is adjusted to form a loop. This loop is tightened by pulling on the ends of the yarn. The knot should be loose enough to slide the hook through it but firm enough not to come undone.

In diagrams, the slip knot is often depicted as a dot or a small circle at the beginning of the base chain. This representation symbolizes the starting point.

Learning how to tie a slip knot is a critical step, as a poorly made knot results in difficulties later on, especially when it comes to maintaining the correct yarn tension.

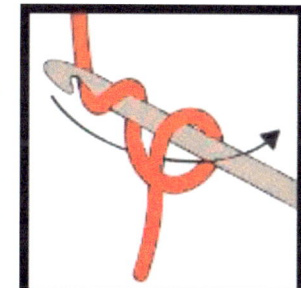

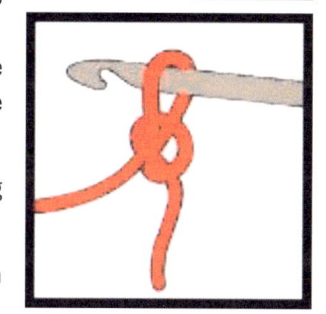

STEP-BY-STEP GUIDE TO MAKING A SLIP KNOT

1. Start by laying the yarn flat on a surface, ensuring you have at least 6 inches of the tail end of the yarn closest to you and the working yarn (the yarn attached to the skein) extending away from you. This setup is crucial for creating a slip knot that can be easily adjusted and doesn't tighten prematurely.

2. Pick up the yarn about 5 to 6 inches from the tail end between your thumb and forefinger of your dominant hand. This measurement is important as it provides enough yarn to form the slip knot without wasting material.

3. Make a loop by crossing the working yarn over the end of the yarn.

4. With the hook in your right hand, pull it under the loop.

5. Once it's under the loop, hook the working yarn.

6. Holding the end of the yarn with your left hand, pull the working yarn with the hook. This will cause the loop to close around, forming the slip knot.

7. Pull the end of the yarn to adjust the size of the slip knot. It should be neither too tight nor too loose; Find a balance that allows the hook to move.

To achieve a perfect slip knot, it is important to maintain an even tension in the yarn. If the knot is too tight, you'll have a hard time inserting the hook into the following chains. On the other hand, a knot that is too loose results in a messy job. Practice will help you find the right tension.

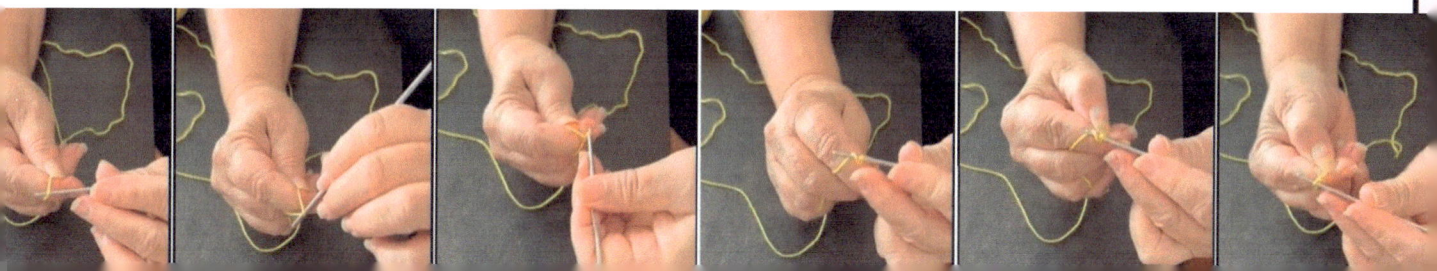

COMMON MISTAKES AND HOW TO AVOID THEM

Creating a slip knot seems straightforward, yet it's common for beginners to encounter a few hiccups along the way. Recognizing and avoiding these common mistakes can ensure a smoother start to your crochet projects.

Mistake 1: Making the Knot Too Tight

A very tight slip knot can make it difficult to insert the hook and work the first stitches. To avoid this, pull the knot snugly around the hook but ensure you can still slide it easily. The knot should comfortably sit on the hook without squeezing it.

Mistake 2: Confusing the Tail and Working Yarn

Sometimes, beginners might pull on the tail end instead of the working yarn when tightening the slip knot, which can lead to unraveling. Remember, the working yarn is the one connected to the skein. After forming the loop, ensure you're pulling on the working yarn to adjust the size of the loop on your hook.

Mistake 3: Knot Placement Too Far from the Hook End

Placing the slip knot too far up the hook shaft can lead to inconsistent tension in your starting chain. Aim to form the knot about an inch from the hook end. This position allows for better control and ease of movement as you begin to crochet.

Mistake 4: Looping the Yarn Incorrectly

For a slip knot to work correctly, the loop must be able to tighten and loosen as needed. Ensure you loop the yarn over itself so that pulling the working yarn tightens the loop. If the loop doesn't tighten or loosen easily, it might not be looped correctly. Practice looping the yarn over your fingers until the mechanism of the slip knot becomes clear and intuitive.

CHAIN STITCH (CH)

Called "chains," they are the basis of almost all works. They are a series of loops that are formed using the hook and yarn. These are the most basic stitches and are used to create the foundation on which others are built.

The chain stitches create what is known as the "foundation row." To do this, after forming the slip knot, perform a "yarn over" and then thread this yarn through the loop on the hook. This process is repeated to form a series of chains, which vary in number depending on the design.

The number of chains in the base row will determine the width of the job. For example, a wider scarf will require more chains in its base row.

Just as they set the width, they serve as the foundation for building other projects. Once the foundation row has been completed, others are worked on these chains.

The way in which the subsequent ones are worked in this foundation row varies depending on the pattern and type used. For example, some patterns require skipping certain chains to create a specific design, while others use each chain to get a denser, more uniform texture.

In diagrams, it is represented by an oval or a small circle. These ovals are shown in sequence to indicate the length of the chain. The chain is the basis for almost all projects and their correct execution to maintain uniformity and proper tension.

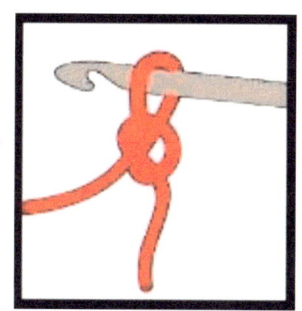

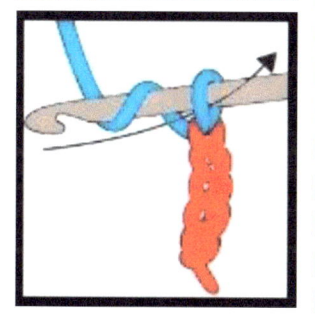

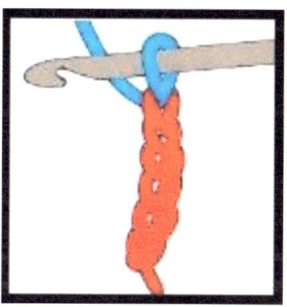

CHAIN STITCH STEP-BY-STEP

1. Start with a slip knot on your hook.

2. Hold the hook in your right hand and the yarn in your left hand (reverse if you're left-handed). The yarn should remain taut, but not too tight.

3. Bring it under and then over the yarn (making a yarn over).

4. With the yarn taken, pull the hook through the loop of the slip knot. This movement creates your first chain stitch.

The same process continues; thread the hook under and over the yarn and then pull through the existing loop. Each repetition forms a new chain. Remember to maintain a consistent tension on the yarn to achieve even chain stitches. If the chain looks too tight or too loose, adjust your grip on the yarn or the hook.

Keep a count of the chains so that you have the necessary amount according to your pattern. The first loop on the hook is not counted as a stitch.

Once you've reached your desired length, you start working on the next row with the stitch you choose, based on your pattern.

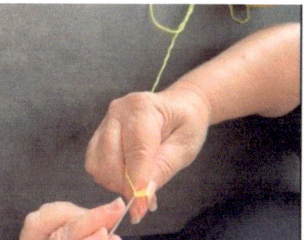

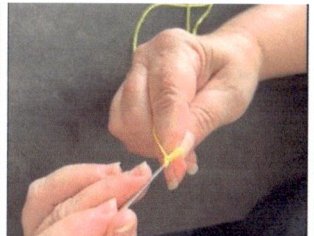

COMMON MISTAKES AND HOW TO AVOID THEM

Maintaining even tension in crochet is crucial for creating uniform stitches and ensuring your project measures up correctly. Here are practical tips to help you achieve consistent tension and avoid common mistakes:

1. Hold Your Yarn Correctly: Wrap the yarn over your pinkie finger and under your ring and middle fingers, then over your index finger. This method provides control over the yarn tension as it feeds through your fingers to the crochet hook.

2. Grip Your Hook Comfortably: Whether you prefer the pencil or knife grip, ensure your hold is relaxed. A tight grip on the hook can lead to uneven stitches and hand fatigue.

3. **Practice Consistent Yarn Feed:** The way you feed the yarn into your stitches affects tension. Aim for a smooth, consistent flow of yarn. Adjust the tension by tightening or loosening the yarn wrap around your fingers.

4. Check Your Stitches Regularly: Every few stitches, pause and check your work. Look for stitches that are too tight or too loose compared to others. Early detection makes it easier to correct tension issues.

5. Adjust Hook Size if Necessary: If you consistently produce tight or loose stitches despite adjusting your grip and yarn tension, consider changing your hook size. A larger hook can help with tight stitches, while a smaller hook can correct loose stitches.

6. Relax Your Shoulders and Hands: Tension in your body translates to tension in your crochet. Take breaks, stretch, and ensure you're working in a comfortable, well-supported position.

7. Practice, Practice, Practice: Like any skill, achieving even tension in crochet comes with time and practice. Work on simple projects to build muscle memory and confidence.

Remember, each crocheter has a unique tension. What's important is consistency throughout your project. If you find your tension varies significantly, unravel and redo the inconsistent section.

FOUNDATION CHAIN

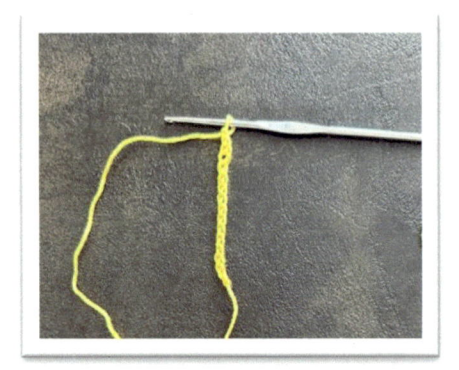

The foundation chain is made up of a series of chain stitches. It gives the initial structure on which the following rows or rounds are built. The length of the foundation chain will determine the width or circumference, so you need to count each one accurately.

To make a foundation chain, start with a slip knot on the hook a few inches from the tail end. Work the foundation chain in a series of yarn overs, pulling the yarn through the previous loop. To work in a foundation chain, insert the hook in the center of the stitch, through the V shape or into the back bump.

Like the chain, the foundation chain is represented in the diagrams with a line of connected ovals. Each oval represents an individual chain stitch. Depending on it, the foundation chain varies in length, from a few chains for small projects to hundreds for larger ones like blankets or shawls.

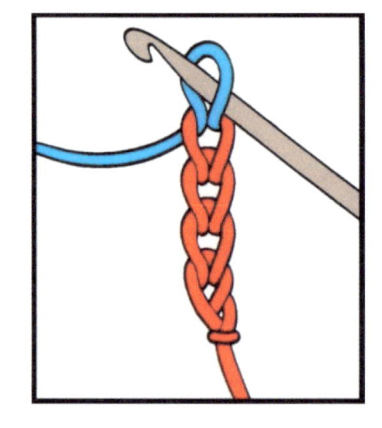

It's important to practice creating an even foundation chain, as a chain that's too tight causes the edge to curve or wrinkle, while a loose chain results in an uneven edge. Consistency in the tension of the foundation chain is crucial to a professional-looking fabric.

TURNING CHAIN (TCH)

The turning chain is a set of chain stitches made at the end of a row before turning the work to start the next row. The function of this chain is to give the necessary height so that the edge of the next row is aligned. The number of chains in your turning chain depends on the stitch you plan to use in the next row. For example, a single crochet typically requires one chain, a half double crochet needs two, a double crochet uses three, and a treble crochet calls for four.

In the diagrams, the turning chain is represented by ovals located at the end of a row. For example, a tall one will be represented by three ovals (indicating three chains) at the end of the row. Remember to make the turning chain, as skipping it results in jagged edges and a decrease in width with each row.

To execute a turning chain, follow these detailed steps:

1. Complete Your Row: Finish the last stitch of your current row according to your pattern.

2. Yarn Over for the Chain: Wrap the yarn over your hook from back to front. This is similar to the yarn over action used in making chain stitches.

3. Pull Through: Pull the yarn through the loop that's already on your hook. This creates one chain stitch.

4. Repeat as Needed: Depending on the stitch for the next row, repeat the yarn over and pull through process the required number of times. For instance, if your next row is a double crochet, you'll make three chains.

5. Turn Your Work: Once your turning chain is complete, turn your work counter-clockwise if you're right-handed, or clockwise if you're left-handed, so the work is positioned for the next row.

6. Begin the Next Row: Start the first stitch of the new row by inserting your hook into the appropriate stitch from the previous row, which may vary based on the pattern you're following.

Remember, the turning chain is not only a functional element but also contributes to the overall appearance of your project. Ensuring that your turning chains are consistent in size and tension with your stitches will help keep your edges neat and professional-looking. Practice making turning chains with different numbers of chains to become comfortable with transitioning between rows of various stitch heights.

CHAIN CIRCLE

The chain circle is a technique used to start circular projects, such as hats, amigurumi, or certain types of rugs. It consists of making a series of chain stitches and then joining the first and last with a slid to form a circle. This circle is a base for working in rounds, allowing you to create circular or spherical shapes.

In diagrams, the chain circle is represented as a series of ovals forming a circle, with a point or line indicating the slide to close the circle. The number of chains will depend on the size of the desired circle and the type used in subsequent rounds.

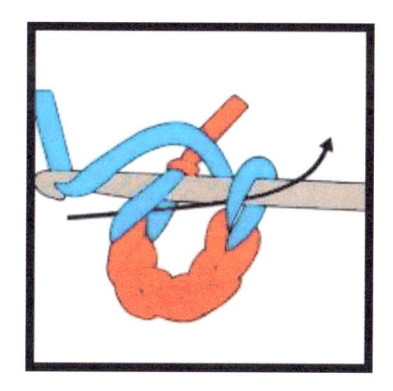

It's important to maintain even tension when creating the chain circle so that its center isn't too tight or loose.

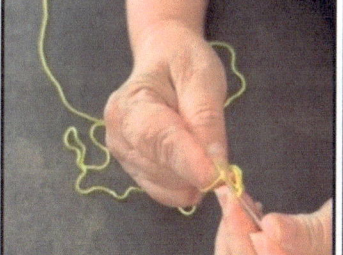

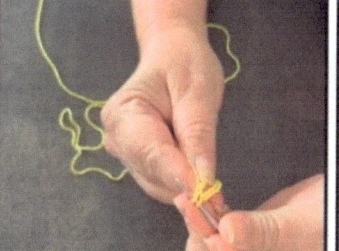

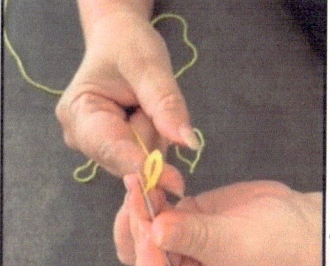

MAGIC RING

The magic ring, known as a magic circle or adjustable ring, is a technique that allows you to adjust the size of the center of the circle after you have worked the first stitches. This method is particularly useful for amigurumi, hats, and any project worked in the round where you don't want a hole at the beginning.

To form a magic ring, wrap the yarn around your fingers to form a loop, insert the hook into the loop, and then work the first stitches of the round into that loop. Once this step is completed, pull the end of the yarn to close the loop and adjust the circle's center.

The ability to adjust the size of the center after working the first ones makes the magic ring such a valuable technique.

PARTS OF THE STITCH

Understanding the parts of a stitch is important for every weaver.

The stitch consists of three main parts: the head, the body and the base. They work all together to form the structure and texture.

Head

It's the top section, and it's the most recognizable part when you look at a piece. It is characterized by its "V" shape and is where the loops of yarn meet and intertwine. This part is the one that is most seen and felt when touching the finished fabric. The precision when working on the head determines uniformity and consistency, affecting both aesthetics and the final texture.

Base

This part is the anchor point that holds the stitches together; it's where you insert the hook to start a new one, and its location varies depending on the type you're making.

At a single crochet, for example, you'll insert the hook under both loops of the "V" on the head in the previous row. In more advanced techniques you could insert around the body, thus creating different textures and visual effects.

The base is critical in determining alignment and structure. Correct insertion into the base ensures that the pattern remains consistent and that each stitch is formed correctly. The base is to maintain structural integrity, that the stitches do not fall apart, and that the work maintains its shape.

Body

It is the vertical section that extends from the base to the head. At different types of stitches, such as low or high, the body varies in length, which affects height and texture. In taller ones the body is longer, resulting in a more flexible fabric with more space between the rows.

It is for shaping, as its length and thickness contribute to the density and elasticity of the final work. The way you handle the body during weaving affects overall tension, an important factor in achieving consistency.

HOW TO COUNT STITCHES

Counting the stitches and chains in the right way ensures that your work will have the desired shape and size. If you skip a stitch or add too many, your work may turn out too large, small or irregularly shaped. Learning to count will allow you to follow patterns with confidence and create accurate and beautiful projects.

To do this, take into account the following steps:

- **Identify the First Stitch**: After making a chain when turning your work, the first one will be right next to the crochet hook; do not confuse the loop on your hook with the actual first stitch.
- **Identify the V-shape:** Each crochet stitch at the top looks like a "V". This V-shape is what you're counting as one stitch. It's important to look closely at your work and identify these V-shapes along the top edge of your crochet fabric.
- **Use Bookmarks**: If you find it difficult to keep track of large or complex jobs, these are a great help. Place a marker at specific stitches (e.g., every 10 or 20) to make it easier to follow.
- **Mark the First and Last Stitch**: For beginners, it can be helpful to place a stitch marker in the first and last stitch of your row or round. This practice makes it easier to see where each row or round starts and ends, reducing the risk of losing or adding stitches unintentionally.
- **Counting in the Round**: When working in rounds, it's crucial to mark the beginning of your round with a stitch marker. Move this marker up as you complete each round. This technique helps you keep track of your rounds and makes counting stitches easier.
- **Check Your Pattern**: Some patterns include a specific number of stitches you should have at the end of a row or round. Use this information to check your work. If your count doesn't match the pattern, double-check your stitches to find where you might have made a mistake.
- **Practice with Scrap Yarn**: If you're new to counting stitches or find it challenging, practice with some scrap yarn. Crochet a small swatch, practicing counting stitches as you go.

Before you begin, practice counting on small samples. This will help you become familiar with the technique and gain confidence in your ability to count accurately. At first, it's a bit tricky, and you might make mistakes. Don't be discouraged. Constant practice will help you improve, and soon counting will come naturally to you.

TIPS FOR MAINTAINING AN EVEN TENSION

Maintaining an even tension is crucial for creating uniform stitches and ensuring your crochet projects look neat and professional.

Here are specific tips to help you achieve consistent tension:

1. **Find Your Comfort Zone with Yarn Handling:** Experiment with different ways of holding the yarn. Some crocheters wrap the yarn around their fingers, while others may simply let it glide over. The key is to find a method that allows you to control the yarn's tension comfortably. For instance, try wrapping the yarn around your pinkie finger once and then over your index finger, adjusting the wrap to increase or decrease tension.

2. **Consistent Yarn Feed:** Ensure the yarn feeds smoothly from the skein or ball. Use a yarn bowl or a bag to keep your yarn tangle-free and rolling smoothly. This prevents sudden changes in tension caused by tugs or snags.

3. **Adjust Grip on the Hook:** Your hook grip impacts tension. A relaxed grip on the hook allows for more fluid movement and consistent stitch size. If you notice your stitches are too tight or too loose, try adjusting your grip. Loosen your grip if stitches are tight; tighten it slightly if stitches are too loose.

4. **Always Use the Same Size of the Hook**, as changing hooks alters the tension and size.

5. If you notice that the tension is not right or that you have made a mistake, do not hesitate to undo it and try again. It's a normal part of the learning process.

NOTE: The best way to achieve even tension is through regular practice. Over time, you'll develop a natural sense for maintaining the right tension.

CHAPTER 4
BASIC STITCHES

Mastering the basic stitches in crochet is akin to learning the alphabet for language; it's the foundation upon which all crochet projects are built. These stitches vary in complexity and texture, offering a wide range of possibilities even for the beginner.

As you become more familiar with these stitches, you'll start to see how they can be combined and adapted to create various textures and patterns. By mastering these seven essential stitches and their variations, you've equipped yourself with the skills needed to crochet many projects.

Let's dive into the seven stitches that are essential for any crocheter to know.

SLIP STITCH (SL ST)

The slip stitch is an essential crochet technique used to join pieces together, create edges, or work in rounds without adding height to the project. It's the shortest of all crochet stitches and is often used for shaping or as a method to move across a piece of crochet work invisibly.

Here's how to make a slip stitch:

1. Insert the Hook: Begin by inserting your crochet hook into the stitch where you want to make the slip stitch. This could be a stitch from the previous row, a space within the crochet fabric, or into a chain stitch.

2. Yarn Over: With the hook inserted into the correct stitch, yarn over by bringing the yarn from back to front over the hook.

3. Pull Through: Gently pull the hook back through the stitch while carrying the yarn through the stitch. You should now have two loops on your hook: the original loop and the one you just pulled through the stitch.

4. Complete the Stitch: Now, pull the loop you just brought through the stitch directly through the loop that was already on your hook. This action leaves you with one loop on the hook and completes the slip stitch.

Tips for Success:

- **Tension:** Keep your tension even but not too tight. A slip stitch that's too tight can be difficult to work into on subsequent rows.
- **Hook Position:** Ensure your hook is facing downwards as you pull through the loops to make it easier.

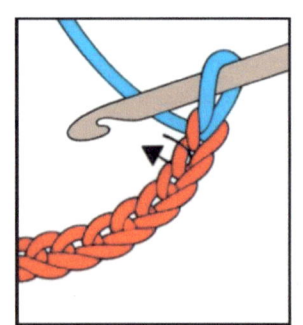

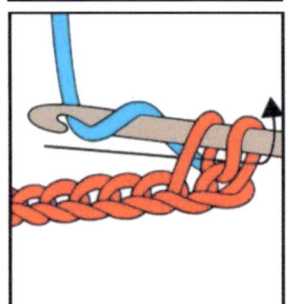

SINGLE CROCHET (SC)

Single crochet is a fundamental stitch and it is the building block for many crochet patterns and projects.

1. Start with a Foundation Chain: Make a foundation chain of the desired length for your project. Remember, the single crochet stitch starts from the second chain from your hook.

2. Insert the Hook: Insert your crochet hook into the second chain from the hook. Ensure the hook goes under both the top and back loop of the chain stitch for a stronger edge.

3. Yarn Over: With the hook inserted into the chain, wrap the yarn over the hook from back to front.

4. Pull Through: Gently pull the hook back through the chain stitch. You will now have two loops on your hook.

5. Yarn Over Again: Wrap the yarn over the hook once more, from back to front.

6. Complete the Stitch: Pull the hook with the yarn through both loops on the hook. You've now completed a single crochet stitch.

7. Continue the Row: Repeat steps 2 through 6 in each chain across the foundation chain. At the end of the row, you should have one loop left on your hook.

8. Turning Your Work: To create multiple rows, you'll need to turn your work. Make one chain stitch (this acts as a turning chain), then turn your work so you can start the next row. Insert the hook into the first stitch of the previous row and repeat steps 3 through 6.

Tips for Success:
- Keep your tension consistent to ensure even stitches and a uniform fabric.
- Count your stitches at the end of each row to keep your edges straight.
- Practice making single crochet stitches evenly and consistently for a neat finish.

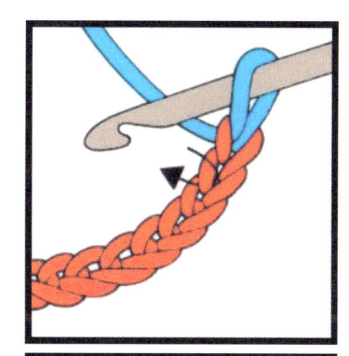

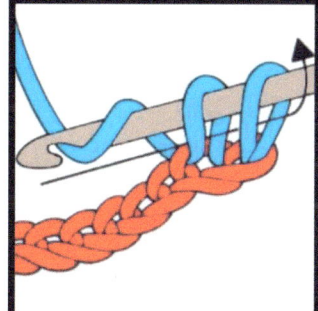

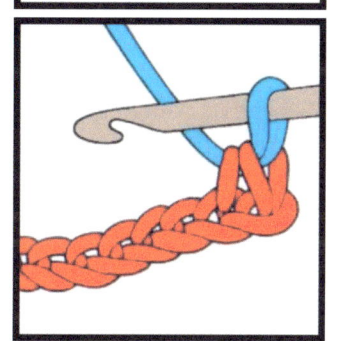

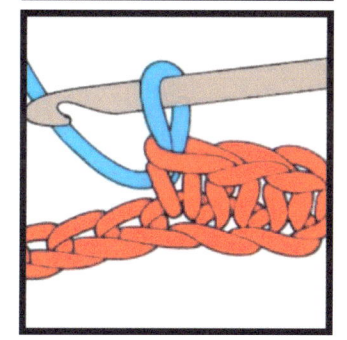

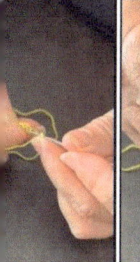

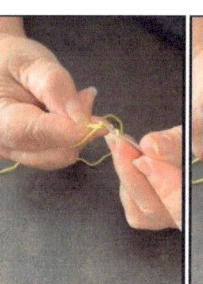

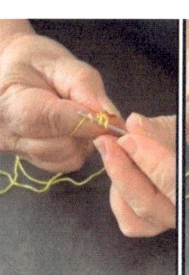

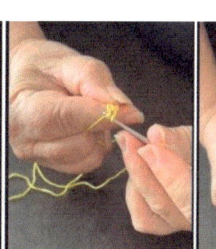

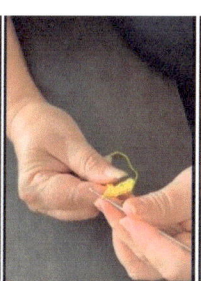

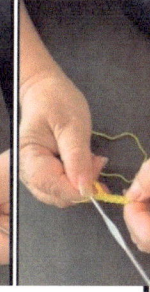

EXTENDED SINGLE CROCHET (ESC)

Extended single crochet elevates the classic single crochet stitch by adding height without the bulkiness of taller stitches. This stitch is perfect for adding subtle texture and a refined look to your projects.

Here's how to create an Extended Single Crochet:

1. Start with a Foundation Chain: Begin by making a foundation chain to the desired length for your project.

2. Insert the Hook: Insert your crochet hook into the second chain from the hook.

3. Yarn Over: Wrap the yarn over your hook from back to front.

4. Pull Up a Loop: Pull the hook through the chain. You will now have two loops on your hook.

5. Yarn Over and Pull Through One Loop Only: This is the additional step that differentiates the ESC from a regular single crochet. Instead of yarning over and pulling through both loops on the hook, yarn over and pull through just the first loop on your hook. You will still have two loops on your hook after this step.

6. Complete the Stitch: Yarn over again and pull through both loops on your hook. You have now completed an Extended Single Crochet stitch.

7. Repeat: Continue to insert your hook into the next chain or stitch, and repeat steps 3 through 6 for each Extended Single Crochet across your foundation chain.

Tips for Success:

- Keep your tension consistent to ensure even stitches and a uniform fabric.
- Practice the stitch on a small swatch before starting a larger project to become comfortable with the motions.
- Use this stitch to add a decorative edge to projects or within the body of a piece for subtle texture.

HALF DOUBLE CROCHET (HDC)

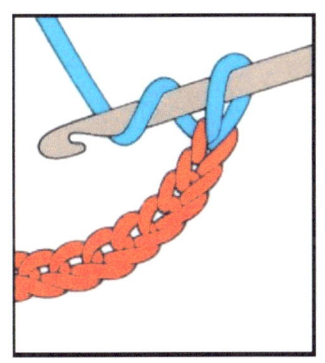

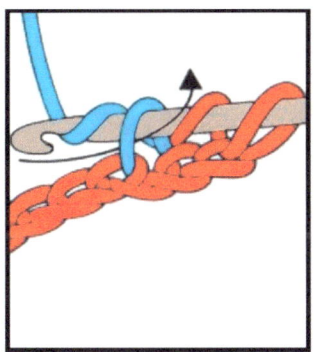

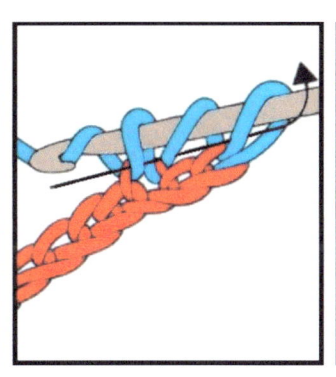

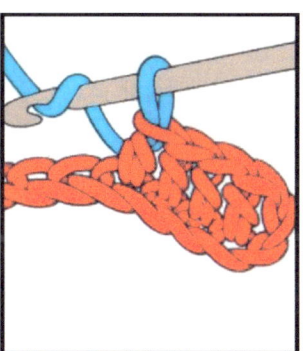

The half double crochet stitch is a versatile and essential stitch that creates a slightly taller and looser fabric than the single crochet, making it perfect for projects that require a balance between density and flexibility, such as hats, scarves, and blankets.

Here's how to make a half double crochet stitch:

1. Yarn Over: Start by wrapping the yarn over the hook from back to front before inserting the hook into your work. This is your first yarn over and is crucial for creating the half double crochet's additional height.

2. Insert the Hook: Identify the stitch where you want to place your half double crochet. Insert your hook into that stitch, going under both loops of the stitch on the row below unless your pattern specifies otherwise.

3. Yarn Over Again: With the hook inserted into the stitch, wrap the yarn over the hook a second time. You now have three loops on your hook: the initial loop, the loop from inserting the hook into the stitch, and the loop from your second yarn over.

4. Pull Through: Pull the hook back through the stitch, bringing the second yarn over through the stitch. Be careful to keep all three loops on your hook as you pull through. You should still have three loops on your hook after this step.

5. Final Yarn Over: Wrap the yarn over the hook once more. This is your final yarn over for the half double crochet stitch.

6. Complete the Stitch: Pull the hook with the yarn through all three loops on your hook in one motion. This completes your half double crochet stitch.

7. Repeat: To continue making more half double crochet stitches, simply repeat steps 1 through 6 in each stitch across your row or round.

Tips for Success:

- Maintain a consistent yarn tension to ensure your stitches are even in size.
- Count your stitches regularly to keep track of your project's dimensions.

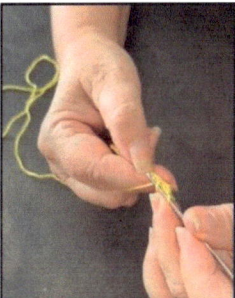

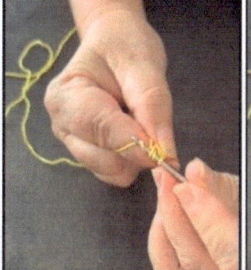

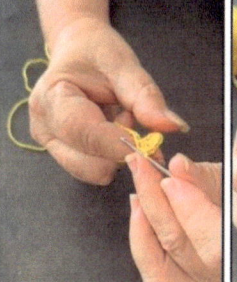

DOUBLE CROCHET (DC)

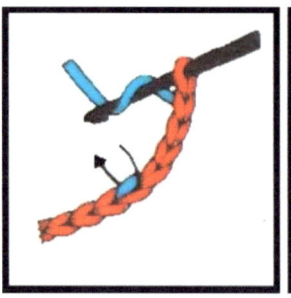

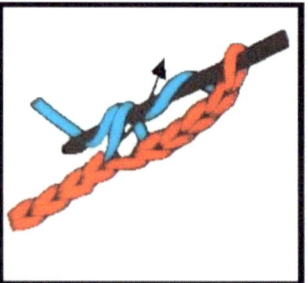

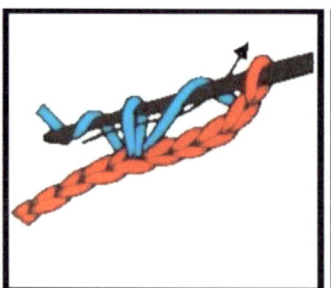

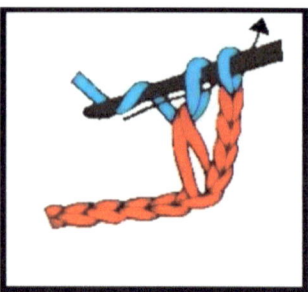

The double crochet stitch is a fundamental crochet technique that creates a relatively tall and airy fabric. This stitch is beloved for its versatility and is used in a wide variety of projects, from blankets and scarves to hats and sweaters. The double crochet offers a great balance between the tightness of a single crochet and the lofty height of more advanced stitches like the treble crochet. It works up faster than the single crochet, making it a popular choice for larger projects.

Here's a detailed step-by-step guide to mastering the double crochet stitch:

1. Start with a foundation chain. For practicing the double crochet, make a chain of any length, but remember that for double crochet, you typically need to chain three extra at the beginning of your row, which counts as the first double crochet stitch.

2. Yarn over the hook. This means you wrap the yarn from back to front over your crochet hook, preparing to insert it into the foundation chain.

3. Insert the hook into the fourth chain from the hook. The extra chains you skipped count as the first double crochet. Inserting the hook into the fourth chain creates the height needed for the double crochet stitch.

4. Yarn over the hook again, then pull the yarn through the chain. You should now have three loops on your hook. This step starts forming the base of the double crochet stitch.

5. Yarn over the hook once more and pull through the first two loops on your hook. Now, you will have two loops remaining on your hook.

6. Yarn over the hook again and pull through the last two loops on your hook. You have now completed one double crochet stitch.

7. To continue, yarn over the hook and insert it into the next chain or stitch, repeating steps 4 through 6. Keep working double crochets into each chain or stitch across your foundation chain for a full row of double crochet stitches.

Tips for Success:

- Ensure that your yarn over and hook movements are consistent in tension and fluidity to maintain even stitch sizes throughout your project.
- Count your stitches at the end of each row to ensure you have the correct number. This is crucial for keeping the edges of your work straight.

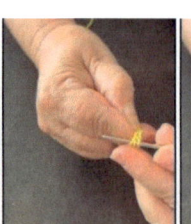

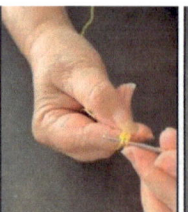

TREBLE CROCHET (TR)

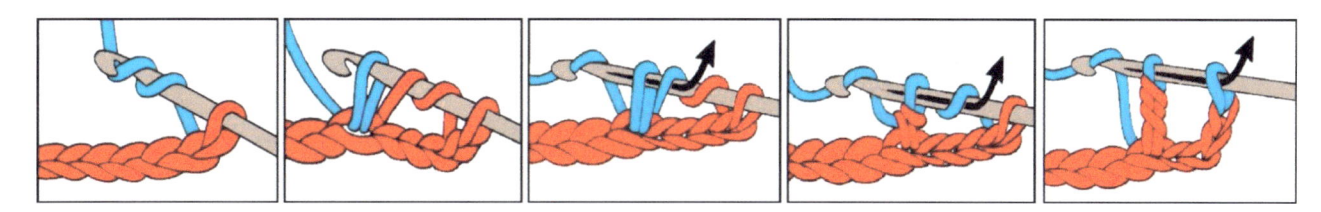

Treble crochet creates a tall and airy fabric, making it ideal for projects that require a lighter texture or faster growth in length. This stitch is taller than the double crochet and it works up quickly, making it a favorite for larger projects or any work where a delicate, open fabric is desired. It's perfect for shawls, afghans, and lightweight garments.

Here's how to execute a treble crochet with precision:

1. Begin with a foundation chain of any length. To practice treble crochet, a chain of 21 is a good starting point, as it allows room for multiple stitches and turning.

2. Yarn over the hook twice. This is the preparatory action for creating the height of the treble crochet.

3. Insert the hook into the fifth chain from the hook. The four chains you skip count as the first treble crochet stitch and provide the necessary height.

4. Yarn over the hook again and pull it through the chain. You will now have four loops on your hook, setting the stage for the treble stitch.

5. Yarn over and pull through the first two loops on the hook. This reduces the number of loops on the hook to three.

6. Yarn over again and pull through the next two loops. At this point, you will have two loops remaining on your hook.

7. Yarn over one last time and pull through the final two loops on your hook. You have now completed a treble crochet stitch.

8. To continue, yarn over twice and insert the hook into the next chain or stitch. Repeat steps 4 through 7 for each stitch across your foundation chain.

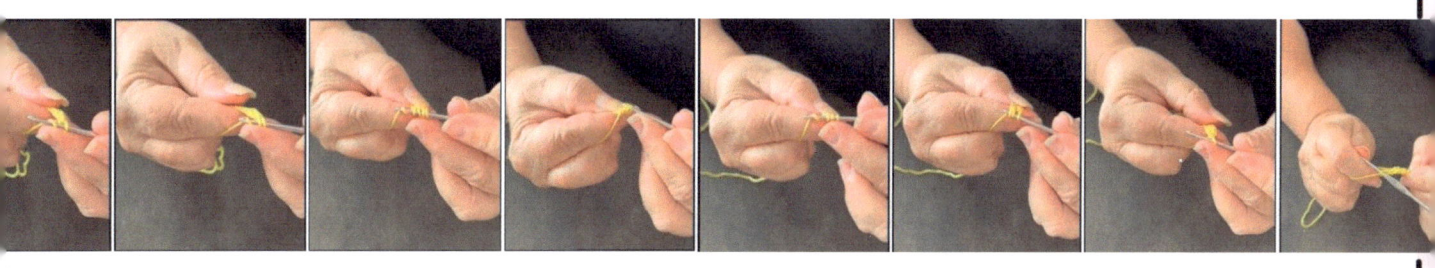

DOUBLE TREBLE CROCHET (DTR)

The double treble crochet stitch offers a generous height and a luxurious drape to your projects. Ideal for airy throws, delicate shawls, and any work where a fluid, open texture is desired, mastering this stitch opens up new avenues for creativity and design in your crochet endeavors.

Step-by-Step Instructions:

1. Start with a Foundation Chain: Begin by creating a foundation chain to the desired length of your project. Remember, the double treble crochet stitch will add significant height, so plan your chain length accordingly.

2. Yarn Over Three Times: Hold the yarn and wrap it over your hook three times. This preparatory step is crucial for achieving the characteristic height of the dtr stitch.

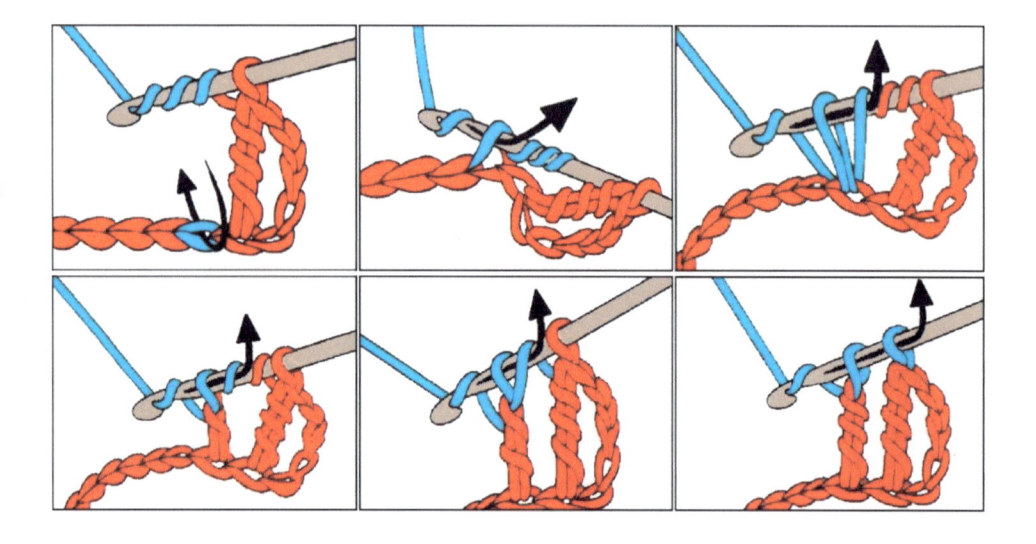

3. Insert Hook: Identify the stitch in your foundation chain where you want to place your first dtr. Counting from the hook, skip the number of chains recommended for your project (usually five for a starting edge) and insert your hook into the next chain.

4. Yarn Over and Pull Through: With the hook inserted into the correct chain, yarn over once more and gently pull through the chain. You will now have five loops on your hook, setting the stage for the formation of the dtr.

5. Yarn Over and Pull Through Two Loops: This action is repeated three times. First, yarn over and carefully pull through the first two loops on your hook. Repeat this step twice more, each time reducing the number of loops on your hook by two, until only one loop remains.

6. Repeat for Subsequent Stitches: Continue to create additional dtr stitches across your foundation chain, following steps 2 through 5. Ensure each stitch is worked with consistent tension for an even and professional finish.

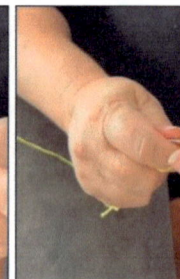

REVERSE SINGLE CROCHET

Unlike others, this one is worked from left to right if you are right-handed, or from right to left if you are left-handed.

1. Insert the hook into the new stitch you just completed, seeing that the thread is behind.

2. Hook the yarn and pull it through the stitch, getting a loop on the hook (you will now have two loops).

3. Hook the yarn once more and thread it through both loops on the hook.

4. Continue this process along the row to create a trimmed, decorative texture.

HOW TO CHANGE COLOR AND WORK IN STRIPES

The ability to incorporate different colors revitalizes a design and makes your creations stand out.

Here are the steps to change color:

1. Start working the last stitch with the current color. So, wrap the yarn and pull the hook through the stitch at the base, pull out the yarn, and pull through the first two loops on the hook. You'll have two loops left.
2. Instead of completing the last step of the stitch with the old color, take the yarn of the new color. Hold the end of the new color along with the yarn in use to hold it in place.
3. With the new color already on the hook, pull it through the last two loops on the hook.
4. Start the next row or round with the new color, following the pattern you're working with.

This is how you work in stripes:

1. Before you start, plan what you want your stripes to look like—the same size or different widths. This will determine how many rows you do with each color before switching.
2. Work the desired number of rows with the first color. For example, if you want stripes that are two rows high, crochet two full rows with the first color.
3. Use the method described above to change color at the end of the last row of the first color.
4. Crochet the number of planned rows with the new color before switching again.
5. Continue alternating colors following your set pattern until you reach the desired length of your project.

Experiment with different color combinations and stripe widths to customize your creations and make them unique.

METHODS OF INCREASE AND DECREASE

Methods of increasing and decreasing are fundamental techniques in crochet that allow you to shape your projects. Whether you're aiming to create a hat, a sweater, or even a simple dishcloth, understanding how to properly add or remove stitches will enable you to achieve the desired size and form.

INCREASING STITCHES

To increase in crochet means to add more stitches to your row or round, which makes your work wider or larger. This is often used in patterns to shape garments or to create motifs.

1. **Identify Where to Increase:** Most patterns will specify where an increase is needed. If you're following a specific design, look for these instructions. If you're improvising, decide where your piece needs to widen.

2. **Making an Increase:** The most common method to increase is to work two stitches into the same stitch from the previous row or round. Here's how you do it:

- Insert your hook into the stitch where you need to increase.
- Yarn over (wrap the yarn over your hook from back to front) and pull up a loop. You now have two loops on your hook.
- Yarn over again and pull through both loops on your hook. You've made one single crochet.
- Insert your hook into the same stitch you just worked into.
- Repeat the steps to make another single crochet in the same stitch. You have now increased by one stitch.

Tips for Increasing:

- Ensure that your increases are evenly spaced out according to your pattern or project needs. This helps maintain a symmetrical shape.
- Use a stitch marker to mark the first increase in a round or row to keep track of where your increases are made.

DECREASING STITCHES

Decreasing reduces the number of stitches in your row or round, which is essential for tapering or shaping your project.

1. **Identify Where to Decrease:** Identify the stitches you'll need to join; the pattern will indicate that you make a decrease, often noted as "sc2tog" for single crochet, for example. If you're working without a pattern, plan your decreases to shape your project as desired.

2. **Making a Decrease:** The most common method to decrease in crochet is to work two stitches together, effectively turning them into one stitch. Here's a step-by-step for a single crochet decrease:

- Insert your hook into the next stitch.
- Yarn over and pull up a loop. Instead of completing the stitch, you'll have two loops on your hook.
- Insert your hook into the next stitch (the one after the stitch you just worked into).
- Yarn over and pull up another loop. You now have three loops on your hook.
- Yarn over and pull through all three loops on your hook. You've just combined two stitches into one, decreasing your stitch count by one.

Tips for Decreasing:

- To keep your work looking neat, try to make your decreases on the wrong side of your work if your project has a right and wrong side. This can make the decreases less noticeable.
- Just like with increases, use stitch markers if needed to mark the beginning of your decrease rounds or rows to easily keep track of your work.

4 BASIC STITCH PATTERNS TO TRY

BASIC SINGLE CROCHET PATTERN SQUARE

DIFFICULTY LEVEL: Beginner
FINISHED MEASUREMENT: A square of 4x4 inches, perfect for practicing and creating a simple coaster.
COLORS: Any solid color for clear visibility of stitches, preferably light shades such as soft blue, gentle pink, or light grey.

GAUGE:

- 4 single crochet stitches = 1 inch
- 4 rows = 1 inch

MATERIALS:

- Medium weight yarn (Worsted)
- Size H-8 (5mm) crochet hook
- Scissors
- Tapestry needle

ABBREVIATIONS USED:
ch = chain
sc = single crochet

STEP-BY-STEP INSTRUCTIONS:

1. Start with a Slip Knot:

- Create a loop with your yarn, ensuring the tail end is behind the working yarn.
- Insert your hook through the loop, grab the working yarn (not the tail), and pull it through the loop.
- Tighten the loop around your hook but not too tightly; it should move freely.

2. Making the Foundation Chain:

- Hold your slip knot and yarn as comfortable for you, ensuring tension is even but not too tight.
- Yarn over (wrap the yarn over your hook from back to front) and pull through the loop on your hook. This creates one chain stitch.
- Repeat this step for 15 chains (ch 15). This will be the foundation of your project.

3. First Row of Single Crochet:

- Insert your hook into the second chain from the hook (the loop on the hook does not count).
- Yarn over and pull up a loop. You should have two loops on your hook.
- Yarn over again and pull through both loops on the hook. This completes one single crochet (sc).
- Continue to make one sc in each ch across the row. You will have 14 sc.

4. Turning Your Work:

- Once you reach the end of the row, ch one (this acts as a turning chain).
- Turn your work so you can start the next row.

CONTINUED →

5. Second and Subsequent Rows:

- Insert your hook under both loops of the first sc of the previous row (not the turning chain).
- Complete a sc stitch as before.
- Continue with sc in each stitch across the row.
- At the end of each row, ch one and turn your work.

6. Repeat for a Total of 14 Rows:

- Continue creating rows until you have a total of 14 rows of sc. This should form a square.

7. Finishing Your Work:

- After completing the last row, cut the yarn, leaving a 6-inch tail.
- Yarn over and pull the tail through the loop on your hook to secure it.
- Use a tapestry needle to weave in the ends on the backside of your work for a neat finish.

BASIC DOUBLE CROCHET PATTERN

DIFFICULTY LEVEL: Beginner

FINISHED MEASUREMENT: Practice swatch: 6 inches by 6 inches (15cm by 15cm)

GAUGE: 4 double crochet stitches per inch (2.5cm) and 4 rows per inch (2.5cm)

MATERIALS:

- Medium weight yarn (Category 4)
- Crochet hook size H-8 (5mm)
- Scissors
- Tapestry needle

ABBREVIATIONS USED:

Ch = Chain
Dc = Double crochet

STEP-BY-STEP INSTRUCTIONS:

1. Start with a Slip Knot: Create a slip knot on your hook. This will be your starting point.

2. Chain Stitches for Foundation Row: Chain 21 stitches (ch 21). This will give you a practice swatch approximately 6 inches wide, depending on your tension. The extra stitch is for turning.

3. First Double Crochet Row: Yarn over the hook, insert the hook into the 4th ch from the hook (the first 3 chains count as your first double crochet). Yarn over again and pull up a loop (3 loops on hook). Yarn over and pull through the first 2 loops on the hook (2 loops remaining). Yarn over again and pull through the remaining 2 loops. This completes your first dc.

4. Continue the Row: Repeat the dc in each ch across the row. You will have 19 dc including the turning chain.

5. Turning Your Work: To start the next row, ch 3 (counts as the first dc of the new row), then turn your work so you can start stitching in the first stitch of the previous row.

6. Subsequent Rows: Yarn over, insert the hook into the next stitch (not the base of the turning chain, as that counts as your first stitch), and complete a dc as before. Continue dc in each stitch across the row.

7. Repeat for Practice: Continue creating rows until your work measures approximately 6 inches in height, matching the width for a square practice swatch. This repetition will help solidify the muscle memory for making double crochet stitches.

8. Finishing Off: Once your swatch is complete, cut the yarn, leaving a tail of about 6 inches. Yarn over and pull through the last loop on your hook completely to secure the end. Weave in this end, as well as any others, with a tapestry needle to give your swatch a finished look.

BASIC HALF DOUBLE CROCHET PATTERN

DIFFICULTY LEVEL: Beginner

FINISHED MEASUREMENT: Sample swatch: 4"x4" (10x10 cm)

GAUGE:

- 14 half double crochet (HDC) stitches x 10 rows = 4"x4" (10x10 cm)
- Gauge is important for ensuring your project sizes correctly. Adjust hook size if necessary to achieve gauge.

MATERIALS:

- Worsted weight yarn (Category 4)
- Size H-8 (5 mm) crochet hook
- Scissors
- Tapestry needle

ABBREVIATIONS USED:

Ch = Chain
Hdc = Half Double Crochet
YO = Yarn Over

STEP-BY-STEP INSTRUCTIONS:

1. Create a Slip Knot: Loop the yarn around your fingers to create a circle, bring the yarn behind the circle, and pull through to create a slip knot. Insert your hook.

2. Ch 15 for the Foundation Chain: YO and pull through the loop on your hook. Repeat 14 more times. You now have 15 ch.

3. Row 1 - Half Double Crochet (hdc):

- YO, insert your hook into the 3rd ch from the hook (the first two ch count as your first hdc).
- YO again and pull up a loop (three loops on hook).
- YO and pull through all three loops on the hook.
- Repeat hdc in each chain across. You will have 13 hdc stitches. Turn your work.

4. Row 2 and Beyond:

- Ch 2 (counts as the first hdc).
- hdc in the next stitch and each stitch across.
- Turn your work at the end of each row.
- Repeat Row 2 until your piece measures 4"x4" (10x10 cm).

5. Finishing:

- After reaching the desired size, cut the yarn, leaving a 6-inch tail.
- YO and pull through the last loop on your hook completely to secure the end.
- Use a tapestry needle to weave in the ends for a neat finish.

BASIC TREBLE CROCHET PATTERN

DIFFICULTY LEVEL: Beginner

FINISHED MEASUREMENT: Sample swatch: 4" x 4" (10 cm x 10 cm)

GAUGE: 15 stitches and 5 rows = 4 inches in treble crochet (tr)

MATERIALS:

- Worsted weight yarn (Category 4)
- Size I-9 (5.5 mm) crochet hook
- Scissors
- Tapestry needle

ABBREVIATIONS USED:
ch = chain
tr = treble crochet
YO = Yarn Over

STEP-BY-STEP INSTRUCTIONS:

1. Start with a Slip Knot: Create a slip knot on your hook. This will be your starting point.

2. Ch 21: YO and pull through the loop on your hook. Repeat 20 more times. This ch will serve as the foundation for practicing the treble crochet stitch.

3. First Tr Row: YO twice, then insert the hook into the 5th ch from the hook. YO and pull up a loop. You should now have 4 loops on your hook.

4. Complete the Stitch: YO and pull through the first 2 loops on your hook. YO again and pull through the next 2 loops. Finally, YO once more and pull through the last 2 loops on your hook. You have now completed one tr.

5. Continue Across: Repeat steps 3 and 4 in each ch across the foundation chain. Remember to start each new row with a ch of 4, which counts as the first tr of the new row.

6. Turning Your Work: At the end of the row, turn your work to start the next row. Ch 4 (counts as the first tr), then YO twice and insert the hook into the second stitch from the hook.

7. Repeat for Practice: Continue practicing by creating several rows of tr. Aim for a square swatch to understand the tension and appearance of your stitches.

8. Finishing Off: Once you've reached your desired size or have practiced enough, cut the yarn, leaving a 6-inch tail. YO and pull the tail through the loop on your hook to secure it. Weave in the ends with a tapestry needle to give your swatch a finished look.

CHAPTER 5
CIRCULAR CROCHET

Circular crochet is a technique that allows you to create projects in the round, such as hats, coasters, and amigurumi toys. This method involves joining stitches in a circle and working around that circle, building layers as you go. Unlike working in rows, circular crochet creates a seamless fabric, perfect for projects that benefit from a continuous structure without the need for sewing seams.

Here's how to get started with circular crochet, focusing on creating a simple coaster as a beginner project:

SIMPLE CIRCULAR COASTER

DIFFICULTY LEVEL: Beginner
FINAL MEASUREMENT: Approximately 4 inches in diameter
GAUGE: Not crucial for this project, but 4 sc = 1 inch can be a guideline

MATERIALS NEEDED:

- Medium-weight yarn (worsted weight) in your choice of color
- Crochet hook size H/8 (5mm)
- Scissors
- Yarn needle for weaving in ends

ABBREVIATIONS USED:

ch = chain
sc = single crochet
sl st = slip stitch

STEP-BY-STEP INSTRUCTIONS:

1. **Start with a Slip Knot:** Make a slip knot on your hook, ensuring the tail end is long enough to weave in later.

2. **Chain 4:** Chain 4 stitches. This small chain will serve as the center of your coaster.

3. **Join to Form a Ring:** Insert the hook into the first ch you made, yarn over, and pull through both the stitch and the loop on your hook to form a ring. You now have the foundation ring for your coaster.

4. **Round 1:** Ch 1 (does not count as a stitch). Work 6 single crochet (sc) stitches into the center of the ring. Join with a slip stitch (sl st) to the first sc to close the round. You should have a total of 6 sc.

5. **Round 2:** Ch 1, then work 2 sc in each stitch around. Join with a sl st to the first sc of the round. You will now have 12 sc.

6. **Round 3:** Ch 1, * work 1 sc in the next stitch, then 2 sc in the following stitch. Repeat from * to around. Join with a sl st to the first sc of the round. This increases your stitch count to 18 sc.

7. **Round 4:** Ch 1, * work 1 sc in each of the next 2 stitches, then 2 sc in the following stitch. Repeat from * to around. Join with a sl st to the first sc of the round. You will have 24 sc.

8. **Continue Increasing:** For a larger coaster, continue the pattern of increasing evenly in each round until you reach the desired size. Each round will increase by 6 stitches.

9. **Finishing:** Once you've reached the desired size, cut the yarn, leaving a tail. Pull the tail through the last loop on your hook and tighten. Use a yarn needle to weave in the ends securely.

TIPS FOR CIRCULAR CROCHET:

- To keep your project flat, ensure you're not increasing too quickly or too slowly. Adjust the number of stitches between increases as needed.
- Use a stitch marker to mark the beginning of each round. This helps you keep track of your progress and ensures you join your rounds correctly.
- If you notice your project starting to cup or ruffle, adjust your tension or the number of increases. Cupping indicates too few increases, while ruffling suggests too many.

TROUBLESHOOTING CIRCULAR CROCHET

Maintaining even rounds in circular crochet is crucial for the aesthetic and structural integrity of your projects. If you notice your work is twisting or curling, it often indicates tension issues or inconsistencies in stitch counts. Here are detailed steps to troubleshoot these common challenges:

1. Check Your Stitch Count Regularly: At the end of each round, pause to count your stitches. Ensuring you have the correct number of stitches is vital to prevent the work from curling. If you find you have too many or too few stitches, carefully unravel to the beginning of the round and correct your stitch count.

2. Maintain Consistent Tension: Uneven tension can cause your work to curl or twist. To achieve consistent tension, hold the yarn so that it can flow freely through your fingers. Adjust your grip on the crochet hook if you find your stitches are too tight or too loose. Practice maintaining a steady rhythm while crocheting to keep your tension even.

3. Use Stitch Markers: Place a stitch marker in the first stitch of each round to keep track of the beginning and end of your rounds. This is especially helpful in projects without a visible seam, as it prevents spiraling and ensures each round is completed fully before moving on to the next.

4. Blocking: If your project is completed and still shows signs of curling or twisting, blocking can help. Wet the finished piece, gently squeeze out excess water (do not wring), and pin it to a blocking mat in the desired shape. Allow it to dry completely. This process can relax the fibers and correct minor curling or shaping issues.

5. Adjust Hook Size: If your work is curling significantly, consider changing your hook size. Curling can occur if the stitches are too tight, suggesting the need for a larger hook. Conversely, if the work is too loose and lacks structure, a smaller hook may be necessary.

6. Practice the Magic Ring for Starting Rounds: For projects that start in the round, such as hats or amigurumi, using the magic ring technique can prevent a hole at the start and ensure a tighter, more even beginning. To make a magic ring, loop the yarn around your fingers to create a circle, insert the hook into the circle, yarn over, and pull up a loop. Then, chain one (or as many as required by your pattern) and work the number of stitches into the ring. Pull the tail to close the circle tightly.

7. Correcting Twisting: If your work begins to twist, it may be due to not turning your work at the end of each round or from working too many or too few stitches into the turning chain. To correct twisting in projects that should remain flat, ensure you are not skipping the first stitch after the chain or working into the slip stitch that closed the previous round unless instructed by the pattern.

8. Review the Foundation Chain: A twisted foundation chain can cause the entire project to twist. Before joining the chain to work in the round, lay it flat on a surface to ensure it is not twisted before making the first round of stitches.

CHAPTER 6
SPECIAL STITCHES

SINGLE CROCHET RIB STITCH

The Single Crochet Rib Stitch creates a stretchy fabric with a texture that resembles the ribs of knitted fabrics, it is ideal for projects that require some flexibility, such as hats, sleeve cuffs, or sweater collars.

STEP-BY-STEP INSTRUCTIONS:

1. Foundation Chain: Start by making a foundation chain of any even number of stitches. This will be the base of your work.

2. Row 1: Single crochet in the second chain from the hook and in each chain across to the end. Turn your work to start the next row. This establishes the base layer for your ribbing.

3. Row 2: Chain 1 (this counts as the first single crochet of the new row). This is your turning chain. Now, instead of inserting your hook under both loops of the next stitch as you normally would for a single crochet, you'll be working into the front and back loops specifically to create the ribbing effect.
- **Front Post Single Crochet (fpsc):** Insert your hook from the front to the back to the front again around the post of the next stitch from the previous row. Yarn over, pull up a loop, yarn over again, and pull through both loops on the hook.
- **Back Post Single Crochet (bpsc):** Insert your hook from the back to the front to the back again around the post of the next stitch. Yarn over, pull up a loop, yarn over again, and pull through both loops on the hook.
- Repeat the fpsc and bpsc across the row, ending with a fpsc on the last stitch.

4. Subsequent Rows: Repeat Row 2 for the pattern. Each row builds upon the last, creating a pronounced ribbed effect as you go.

5. Finishing: Once you've reached your desired length, tie off your work and weave in any loose ends with a yarn needle.

MESH

This mesh stitch creates a lightweight, open fabric that's perfect for market bags, airy scarves, or even lightweight summer tops. The simplicity of the stitch pattern makes it an excellent choice for beginners looking to add texture and visual interest to their projects. The key to a beautiful mesh is maintaining consistent tension throughout your work, ensuring that each chain-1 space is uniform for an even, open look.

STEP-BY-STEP INSTRUCTIONS:

1. Foundation Chain: Begin with a foundation chain in a multiple of 2 + 1 for your desired width. For example, if you want a mesh scarf, you might start with 31 chains (30 for the pattern multiple and 1 extra for the turning chain).

2. Row 1: Single crochet in the second chain from the hook to establish your base. * Chain 1, skip the next chain, single crochet in the next chain. Repeat from * *to* across the row. You will end with a single crochet in the last chain. Turn your work to start the next row.

3. Row 2: Chain 1 (counts as the first single crochet). * Single crochet in the next chain-1 space from the previous row, chain 1. Repeat from * to across, ending with a single crochet in the turning chain from the previous row. Turn your work.

4. Repeat Row 2 for the pattern. Continue building your mesh fabric by repeating Row 2 until you reach your desired length. Each row builds upon the chain-1 spaces from the previous row, creating a consistent mesh pattern throughout.

5. Finishing: Once you've reached the desired length, cut the yarn, leaving a tail. Pull the tail through the last loop on your hook and tighten. Use a yarn needle to weave in the ends securely.

POST STITCHES

Post stitches are a unique and versatile technique in crochet that allows you to add texture and dimension to your projects. They can be used to create ribbing, cables, or textured patterns. Unlike regular stitches that are worked into the top loops of the stitch below, post stitches are worked around the post of the stitch from the previous row.

There are two main types: the front post stitch (fps) and the back post stitch (bps).

FRONT POST STITCH:

1. Yarn over your hook.

2. Insert your hook from the front to the back and then to the front again around the post of the stitch in the previous row. Your hook should go under the stitch and be positioned in front of the work.

3. Yarn over the hook again and pull the yarn through the space around the post (you now have 3 loops on your hook).

4. Yarn over once more and pull through two loops on your hook (2 loops left).

5. Yarn over again and pull through the remaining two loops on your hook. You have now completed a front post double crochet (fpdc).

FOR A BACK POST STITCH, THE PROCESS IS SIMILAR BUT WORKED FROM THE BACK:

1. Yarn over your hook.

2. Insert your hook from the back to the front and then to the back again around the post of the stitch from the previous row. Your hook should go under the stitch and be positioned behind the work.

3. Yarn over the hook and pull the yarn through the space around the post (3 loops on the hook).

4. Yarn over and pull through two loops (2 loops left).

5. Yarn over again and pull through the remaining two loops. You have completed a back post double crochet (bpdc).

V-STITCH

The V-stitch creates a pattern that resembles the letter "V" by combining a series of double crochets and chain spaces. This stitch adds a lovely texture and visual interest to various projects, from blankets to scarves, making it a favorite among beginners and seasoned crocheters alike.

STEP-BY-STEP INSTRUCTIONS:

1. Start with a foundation chain that is a multiple of 3 plus 4 chains to turn.

2. Begin in the fifth chain from the hook. To make your first V-stitch, yarn over and insert the hook into the chain.

3. Yarn over and pull up a loop. You should now have three loops on your hook.

4. Yarn over and pull through two loops. Two loops remain on the hook.

5. Yarn over again and pull through the remaining two loops. This completes one double crochet.

6. Chain 1 for the space in the middle of the V.

7. Make another double crochet in the same chain as the first double crochet to complete the V-stitch.

8. Skip 2 chains, then repeat the V-stitch in the next chain (double crochet, chain 1, double crochet in the same chain).

9. Continue this pattern across the row. At the end of the row, chain 3 and turn to start the next row.

10. For the next and subsequent rows, place each V-stitch in the chain-1 space of the V-stitch from the previous row.

SHELL STITCH

The shell stitch creates a series of arches or "shells" across your crochet work, making it ideal for blankets, scarves, and other cozy items. This stitch combines multiple double crochets into a single stitch from the previous row, creating a shell-like pattern.

STEP-BY-STEP INSTRUCTIONS:

1. Start with a foundation chain; the total number of chains should be a multiple of the stitch count for a single shell plus the turning chain. For a basic shell stitch using 5 double crochets per shell, start with a foundation chain that is a multiple of 5, plus 2 chains for the turning chain.

2. Yarn over and insert the hook into the fifth chain from the hook. The first 4 chains count as your first double crochet and chain 1.

3. Complete a double crochet by yarning over and pulling through two loops on the hook twice. You should now have two loops on your hook.

4. Make 4 more double crochets into the same chain. You have now created your first shell.

5. Skip 4 chains, then single crochet into the next chain to anchor the shell.

6. Skip 4 more chains, then work 5 double crochets into the next chain to create the next shell.

7. Continue this pattern across the row. You will end with a half shell (3 dc) in the last stitch to balance the row.

8. To turn and start the next row, chain 3 (counts as the first double crochet of the new shell), then work 4 double crochets into the same stitch as the turning chain. This creates a half shell at the beginning of the row.

9. Anchor the shell with a single crochet in the top of the shell from the previous row.

10. Continue working shells and anchoring them with single crochets across the row.

PUFF STITCH

The puff stitch is a versatile and textured crochet stitch that adds a fluffy, 3D effect to your projects, perfect for blankets, hats, and scarves. It creates a series of puffs or bobbles that stand out, giving your work a rich texture. Adjust the number of yarn overs to make your puffs larger or smaller, customizing the texture to fit your project's needs.

STEP-BY-STEP INSTRUCTIONS:

1. Yarn Over: Start by yarning over your hook.

2. Insert Hook: Insert your hook into the stitch where you want your puff stitch to be located.

3. Yarn Over and Pull Up a Loop: Yarn over again and pull up a loop. You should have three loops on your hook. Make sure to pull up the loop to a height similar to a double crochet; this is crucial for creating the puffiness.

4. Repeat for Fullness: Repeat steps 1 through 3, yarning over and pulling up a loop in the same stitch, usually three to four more times depending on how full you want your puff stitch to be. Each time adds more loops to your hook.

5. Yarn Over and Pull Through All Loops: After you have the desired number of loops on your hook (typically 7 to 9 loops for a medium puff), yarn over once more and pull through all the loops on your hook in one go.

6. Secure the Puff: To secure the puff and prevent it from unraveling, chain 1. This chain does not count as a stitch in your pattern but acts as a knot to hold the puff stitch in place.

POPCORN STITCH

The popcorn stitch creates a raised, puffy texture reminiscent of popcorn. This stitch is perfect for adding dimension to blankets, scarves, and hats. Remember, the key to a successful popcorn stitch is ensuring that all your double crochets are worked into the same stitch and that you pull the loop through tightly when completing the stitch. This will give you a neat, pronounced popcorn effect.

STEP-BY-STEP INSTRUCTIONS:

1. Start by making a foundation chain of any length, plus one turning chain.

2. Work 4 or 5 double crochets into the same stitch. The number of double crochets will determine the puffiness of your popcorn stitch; 5 double crochets will make a fuller popcorn.

3. Drop the loop from your hook. Insert your hook from front to back through the top of the first double crochet you made.

4. Pick up the dropped loop with your hook and pull it through the stitch.

5. Secure the popcorn stitch by chaining 1. This chain does not count as a stitch in your pattern but locks the popcorn stitch in place.

6. To continue, skip the next stitch on your foundation chain and make one single crochet in the next stitch. This creates a space between your popcorn stitches and allows the texture to stand out.

7. Repeat the process for creating popcorn stitches across your row. At the end of the row, turn your work and start the next row with a turning chain.

PICOT STITCH

The picot stitch is a classic method of adding a decorative border or details to the edges of fabrics, applicable on shawls, blankets, and scarves.

STEP-BY-STEP INSTRUCTIONS:

1. Begin by reaching the point in your project where you want to add a Picot stitch. This could be at the end of a row, within a pattern, or as part of an edging.

2. Chain 3. This forms the basis of your Picot loop. Ensure that your chain stitches are not too tight, as you'll need to work into the first of these chain stitches next.

3. Insert your hook into the third chain from the hook—the first chain stitch you made. This step is crucial for forming the Picot loop.

4. Yarn over and pull through both the chain stitch and the loop already on your hook. This completes the Picot stitch and secures the loop.

5. Continue with your crochet project, either by making more stitches as per your pattern or adding additional Picot stitches at intervals for a decorative edge.

TIPS:

- Consistency is key. Make sure all your Picot stitches are the same size for a uniform look.
- Picot stitches can be spaced according to your project's needs. Experiment with different intervals to achieve the desired effect.

CHAPTER 7
GRANNY SQUARES

The Granny Square is a traditional crochet pattern that combines simplicity and versatility and can be transformed into a variety of projects. From blankets and pillows to bags and scarves, the possibilities are endless. Its structure allows for easy color changes, making it popular for creating colorful and varied designs. It's made up of clusters of three double crochet stitches, separated by spaces and worked in the round.

You can use a single color or change colors to create various designs. For this project, we'll incorporate color changes to add visual interest and practice an essential crochet skill.

BASIC GRANNY SQUARE WITH COLOR CHANGES

STEP-BY-STEP INSTRUCTIONS:

1. Begin by creating a slip knot on your hook.

2. Next, chain 4 (ch 4). This small chain will serve as the center of your Granny Square. Join the chain with a slip stitch into the first chain to form a ring. This creates the space you'll work into for the first round.

3. For the first round, chain 3 (counts as your first double crochet, dc). Work 2 dc into the center ring. This forms your first cluster. Chain 2 to create a corner space. Work 3 dc into the center ring again. Repeat the process of chaining 2 and adding 3 dc clusters two more times. You'll have four clusters and four corner spaces. Join with a slip stitch to the top of the initial chain 3 to close the round.

4. To change colors, cut the yarn, leaving a tail to weave in later. Join the new color yarn with a slip stitch in any corner space. It's a good practice to start in a corner space to maintain the square's shape and symmetry. Chain 3 to count as the first dc of the new round.

5. In the same space, work 2 dc, chain 2, and then 3 dc. This creates the corner. Each corner of the square will follow this pattern: 3 dc, chain 2, 3 dc. Work this pattern in each of the four corners. Between corners, simply chain 1. This single chain creates a space between clusters on each side of the square.

6. To finish your Granny Square, once you've reached the desired size, cut your yarn, leaving a tail long enough to weave in with a yarn needle. Pull the yarn through the last loop on your hook and tighten to secure. Weave in any remaining tails in the back of your work to give your square a neat finish.

CONSIDERATIONS AND RECOMMENDATIONS:

- As you work, you'll notice the square beginning to form. The beauty of the Granny Square lies in its simplicity and the creative potential with color changes. Each round expands the square, adding new dimensions and opportunities for color variation.

- Remember, the key to a neat Granny Square is consistent tension. Keep your stitches even and not too tight. This ensures that your square lays flat and the corners are well-defined.

- As you progress with your Granny Square, the rounds will become larger, and you'll have the opportunity to play with more color combinations. After completing the first few rounds and mastering the corner and side clusters, you're ready to expand your square.

- To do this, simply continue the established pattern of creating corner clusters (3 dc, ch 2, 3 dc) in each corner space and a single cluster (3 dc) in the space between corner clusters from the previous round.

- When adding new colors, consider the overall design of your Granny Square. You might choose a repeating pattern of colors or a random assortment for a more eclectic look.

- To change colors, finish the last stitch of your current color by pulling through the new color on the final yarn over. This technique creates a seamless transition between colors. Weave in ends as you go or leave them until the end for a final tidy-up.

- For those looking to create a larger project from multiple squares, think about how your squares will join together. Some prefer to crochet them together using a slip stitch or single crochet for a raised, textured seam. Others might opt for sewing the squares together with a yarn needle for a flatter seam. Whichever method you choose, laying out your squares before joining them allows you to plan the final appearance of your project.

- As your Granny Square grows, you might find the edges beginning to ripple or curl. This is often a sign of too tight or too loose tension. Take a moment to review your stitches. Are they uniform in size? Adjusting your grip on the hook or the tension of your yarn can help correct this issue.

SOLID GRANNY SQUARE

This style is a variation that fills in the traditional spaces with stitches, making it a denser fabric. It is perfect for those looking for a more solid, warm piece, ideal for blankets or coasters.
Choose your yarn color or a combination of colors.

STEP-BY-STEP INSTRUCTIONS:

1. Begin by making a slip knot and place it on your hook. Chain 4 and join with a slip stitch to form a ring. This will be the center of your square.

2. Chain 3 (this counts as your first double crochet), then make 2 double crochets into the ring. Unlike the traditional Granny Square, you won't chain 1 here. Instead, immediately make 3 more double crochets into the ring to start forming the sides of your square.

3. Continue around the ring, making groups of 3 double crochets with no chain spaces between groups. You'll end with 12 double crochets in total for the first round.

4. For the second round and beyond, chain 3 at the beginning of each round, which counts as the first double crochet. In the corners, you'll make 2 double crochets, chain 2, and 2 more double crochets all in the same space to create the corner. Along the sides, simply make 1 double crochet in each stitch from the previous round, with no chain spaces between. This creates the solid fabric effect.

GRANNY SQUARE WITH A CIRCULAR CENTER

STEP-BY-STEP INSTRUCTIONS:

1. Start with a magic ring, which allows the center hole to be tightened completely. Chain 3 (counts as your first double crochet), then make 11 more double crochets into the ring for a total of 12 double crochets. Pull the ring tight to close the center hole. Join with a slip stitch to the top of the initial chain 3.

2. For the next round, chain 3 (counts as the first double crochet), then make 2 double crochets in each stitch around, resulting in a circle with 24 double crochets.

3. To transition to a square, the following round will create corners by making (2 double crochets, chain 2, 2 double crochets) in one stitch to form a corner, then double crochet in the next few stitches before creating the next corner. This method transforms the circle into a square.

HEXAGON GRANNY SQUARE

STEP-BY-STEP INSTRUCTIONS:

1. Begin with a magic ring to keep the center tight and neat.

2. Chain 3 (counts as the first double crochet) and make two double crochets into the ring. This forms your first cluster.

3. Chain 2 to create the first corner. In the same ring, make another cluster of 3 double crochets and chain 2. Repeat this process four more times for a total of six clusters and six chain-2 spaces, creating the hexagon's corners.

4. Join with a slip stitch to the top of the initial chain 3. For subsequent rounds, start each round with a chain 3 (counts as the first double crochet), followed by two double crochets, chain 2, and three double crochets in each corner space. Make one double crochet in each stitch between corners. This method expands the hexagon while maintaining its shape.

TRIANGLE GRANNY SQUARE

STEP-BY-STEP INSTRUCTIONS:

1. Start with a slip knot and chain 4, joining with a slip stitch to form a ring.

2. Chain 3 (counts as the first double crochet), then make 2 double crochets into the ring, chain 2 to create the first corner, and then make 3 double crochets into the ring.

3. Chain 2 for the second corner, and make 3 more double crochets into the ring, followed by another chain 2 for the third corner. You will have a total of three clusters of 3 double crochets and three chain-2 spaces, forming a triangle.

4. Join with a slip stitch to the top of the initial chain 3.

5. For the next round and any additional rounds, chain 3 to start, then follow the pattern of 2 double crochets, chain 2, and 3 double crochets in each corner space, with a double crochet in each stitch between the corners. This creates a larger triangle while preserving the crisp corners and edges.

GRANNY SQUARE COASTERS

DIFFICULTY LEVEL: Beginner

FINISHED MEASUREMENT: Approximately 4x4 inches

MATERIALS:

- Medium-weight yarn (worsted) in two colors (Color A for the main part, Color B for the border)
- Crochet hook size H/8 (5mm)
- Scissors
- Yarn needle

ABBREVIATIONS USED:

- ch: chai
- sl st: slip stitch
- dc: double crochet
- rnd: round

STEP-BY-STEP INSTRUCTIONS:

1. Starting with Color A, make a slip knot and ch 4. Join with a sl st to form a ring.

2. Rnd 1: Ch 3 (counts as first dc), work 11 dc into the ring. Join with a sl st to the top of the beginning ch 3. You should have 12 dc in total.

3. Rnd 2: Ch 3 (counts as first dc), dc in the same stitch as joining, 2 dc in each stitch around. Join with a sl st to the top of the beginning ch 3. You should have 24 dc in total.

4. Rnd 3: Ch 3 (counts as first dc), * dc in the next stitch, 2 dc in the next stitch. Repeat from * to around. Join with a sl st to the top of the beginning ch 3. You should have 36 dc in total. Fasten off Color A.

5. Switch to Color B for the border. Join Color B with a sl st to any dc.

6. Border Rnd: Ch 1, * sc in the next stitch, ch 3, skip 1 stitch. Repeat from * to around. Join with a sl st to the first sc. Fasten off and weave in ends.

7. Finishing: Use the yarn needle to weave in any loose ends for a neat finish.

GRANNY SQUARE BLANKET

DIFFICULTY LEVEL: Beginner

MATERIALS:

- Medium-weight yarn (worsted) in various colors for the squares and a neutral color for joining and bordering
- Crochet hook size H/8 (5mm)
- Scissors
- Yarn needle for weaving in ends

ABBREVIATIONS USED:

- ch: chain
- sl st: slip stitch
- dc: double crochet
- rnd: round

STEP-BY-STEP INSTRUCTIONS:

1. Selecting Yarn Colors: Choose a palette that matches your decor or personal preference. For a cohesive look, select four to five colors that complement each other and a neutral color for joining the squares and creating the border.

2. Making the Granny Squares:
- Start by creating a slip knot and chaining 4. Join with a sl st to form a ring.
- **Rnd 1**: Ch 3 (counts as the first dc), then make 2 dc into the ring, ch 2. * Make 3 dc into the ring, ch 2. Repeat from * to two more times. Join with a sl st to the top of the beginning ch 3. You should have four 3-dc clusters and four ch-2 spaces.
- **Rnd 2**: Sl st in the next 2 dc and into the ch-2 space to start in a corner. Ch 3 (counts as the first dc), 2 dc in the same space, ch 2, 3 dc in the same space (corner made). * Ch 1, in the next ch-2 space (3 dc, ch 2, 3 dc). Repeat from * to for each side. Join with a sl st to the top of the beginning ch 3.
- Repeat Rnd 2 for the desired number of rounds per square, usually 4-6 rounds depending on the size of the blanket you wish to make.

3. Finishing Squares: Once you have completed the desired number of rounds for each square, cut the yarn, leaving a tail. Pull the tail through the last loop on your hook and tighten to secure. Use a yarn needle to weave in the ends.

4. Lay out your squares in the desired pattern before joining. This allows you to visualize the final blanket and make any necessary adjustments to the color distribution.
- Using the neutral color yarn and a yarn needle or your crochet hook, join the squares by whip stitching or slip stitching the edges together through the back loops only. This method creates a flat, nearly invisible seam.
- Work in one direction first, joining all the squares into rows, and then join the rows together.

5. Adding a Border: Once all squares are joined, you can add a border to unify the blanket and give it a finished look.
- Attach the neutral color yarn in any corner of the blanket with a sl st.
- **Round 1 of Border**: Ch 3 (counts as the first dc), then work dc evenly around the entire blanket, working 3 dc in each corner space to maintain the shape. Join with a sl st to the top of the beginning ch 3.
- For a simple border, repeat Round 1 for 2-3 more rounds or until you reach the desired border width.

CONTINUED

CONSIDERATIONS AND RECOMMENDATIONS:

- As you work on your Granny Square Blanket, remember to maintain consistent tension to ensure that all your squares are the same size and that the blanket lays flat. This project not only allows you to practice making granny squares but also teaches you how to join them and finish a larger project. Keep in mind that the beauty of a granny square blanket lies in its versatility and the endless possibilities for customization through color and layout.

- To ensure your Granny Square Blanket reflects a harmonious blend of colors and patterns, take a moment to review your layout once more before proceeding to the joining phase. This step is crucial for catching any last-minute changes that could enhance the overall aesthetic of your blanket. With your layout finalized, you're ready to move on to the crucial stage of assembling your masterpiece.

FOR THE JOINING PROCESS, IF YOU'VE CHOSEN THE WHIP STITCH OR SLIP STITCH METHOD, HERE'S A MORE DETAILED BREAKDOWN TO GUIDE YOU THROUGH:

1. Begin at the top right corner of your first square. Thread your yarn needle with a length of the neutral yarn, or if you're using a crochet hook, prepare to use a slip stitch.

2. Align the first two squares with the right sides facing up for slip stitching, or facing each other for whip stitching. This ensures that the seam is either invisible or neatly tucked away on the backside.

3. Insert your needle or hook through the back loops of both squares' corresponding stitches. The back loop is the loop furthest away from you. For whip stitching, wrap the yarn over the needle and pull through both loops, moving from right to left across the top of both squares. For slip stitching with a crochet hook, insert the hook, yarn over, and pull through all loops on the hook, working from one corner to the other.

4. Continue this process, ensuring that your stitches are neither too tight nor too loose. A consistent tension will keep the squares aligned without bunching or gaping.

5. Once you reach the end of the first pair of squares, fasten off your yarn, and weave in the ends securely. Then, proceed to the next pair of squares, repeating the process until all squares in a row are joined.

6. After completing all horizontal joins, start joining the rows together vertically using the same method. This step gradually brings your blanket together, revealing the pattern you've meticulously laid out.

FOR A MORE DETAILED BORDER, CONSIDER THESE VARIATIONS:

- **Picot Edge**: After your initial rounds of dc, try incorporating a picot edge for a delicate finish. To do this, * ch 3, sl st in the first ch, skip 1 dc, sl st in the next dc. Repeat from * to around the blanket.

- **Shell Edge**: For a more decorative finish, skip 2 dc, 5 dc in the next dc, skip 2 dc, sl st in the next dc. This creates a beautiful scalloped edge around your blanket.

CHAPTER 8
EASY PROJECTS FOR BEGINNERS

SIMPLE DISHCLOTH

This simple dishcloth project introduces beginners to basic crochet techniques, including creating a slip knot, making a foundation chain, and working the single crochet stitch. The repetitive nature of the single crochet stitch allows for practice and improvement of tension and stitch uniformity.

DIFFICULTY LEVEL: Beginner

FINISHED MEASUREMENT: Approximately 8x8 inches, a standard size for kitchen use.

MATERIALS:

- 100% cotton yarn in your choice of color
- crochet hook size H/8 (5mm)
- scissors
- yarn needle

STEP-BY-STEP INSTRUCTIONS:

1. Start by creating a slip knot.

2. Next, chain 27 stitches (ch 27). This will be the foundation chain, and the number of chains can be adjusted to make the dishcloth larger or smaller. Remember, the initial chain length will determine the width of your dishcloth.

3. For the first row, insert your hook into the second chain from the hook, yarn over, and pull up a loop. You now have two loops on your hook. Yarn over again and pull through both loops on the hook, making a single crochet. Continue to single crochet in each chain across the row. You will have 26 single crochets. Chain 1 and turn your work to start the next row.

4. The second row and all subsequent rows will be worked in single crochet as well. The chain 1 at the beginning of each row does not count as a stitch. Insert your hook into the first single crochet of the previous row, yarn over, and complete a single crochet.

5. Continue with single crochets in each stitch across. At the end of each row, chain 1 and turn. As you work, you will notice the fabric beginning to form. The texture of the single crochet stitch is ideal for dishcloths as it creates a durable and absorbent fabric.

6. Continue crocheting rows of single crochet until the dishcloth measures approximately 8 inches from the beginning. To ensure your dishcloth is square, you can use a ruler or measuring tape to check the dimensions as you crochet.

CONTINUED →

7. When you have reached the desired size, cut the yarn, leaving a tail of about 6 inches. Pull this tail through the last loop on your hook and tighten to secure. Use the yarn needle to weave in this end, as well as any other loose ends on the dishcloth, for a neat finish.

TO ADD A DECORATIVE EDGE and further practice your crochet skills, consider creating a border around the completed dishcloth. This not only enhances the aesthetic appeal but also provides a neat, finished look to your project.

1. Begin the border by attaching the yarn with a slip stitch to any corner of the dishcloth. You might choose a contrasting color for a pop of interest or the same color for a uniform look.

2. For the border, chain 1 to start, then evenly work single crochet stitches around the perimeter of the dishcloth. In each corner, work 3 single crochets into the same stitch to create a smooth, rounded edge. This technique ensures that the corners do not curl and the dishcloth lays flat. As you work your way around, insert the hook through both layers of fabric at the edges to secure the border tightly.

3. Upon reaching the starting point of the border, join the final stitch to the first single crochet with a slip stitch.

4. Cut the yarn, leaving a tail long enough to weave in with your yarn needle.

5. Thread the tail through the needle and weave it in securely back and forth through the stitches on the backside of the dishcloth. This hides any loose ends and ensures that your work does not unravel with use or during washing.

EAR WARMER

This simple yet stylish ear warmer is perfect for beginners and makes a great accessory for chilly days. The medium-weight yarn provides warmth and comfort, while the half double crochet stitch offers a nice texture and stretch for a snug fit.

DIFFICULTY LEVEL: Beginner

FINISHED MEASUREMENT: Approximately 20 inches in circumference and 4 inches in width

MATERIALS:

- Medium-weight yarn (worsted) in your choice of color
- Crochet hook size H/8 (5mm)
- Yarn needle
- Scissors

ABBREVIATIONS USED:

- ch: chain
- hdc: half double crochet
- sl st: slip stitch

STEP-BY-STEP INSTRUCTIONS:

1. Begin by creating a slip knot on your crochet hook. Chain 70 stitches, or enough to wrap comfortably around the head with a slight stretch. This will be the foundation of your ear warmer.

2. Join the chain with a sl st to the first chain to form a circle. Ensure not to twist the chain.

3. Round 1: Ch 1 (does not count as a stitch). Work 1 hdc into the same stitch as the join and each stitch around. Join with a sl st to the first hdc. You should have 70 hdc.

4. Round 2-5: Ch 1 and work 1 hdc in each stitch around. Join with a sl st to the first hdc of each round.

5. After completing the 5th round, cut the yarn, leaving a 6-inch tail. Pull the tail through the last loop on your hook and tighten to secure.

6. Use the yarn needle to weave in the ends on the inside of the ear warmer for a neat finish.

7. Optional: For a decorative touch, you can add a crochet flower or bow on one side of the ear warmer. Use the same or contrasting color yarn to crochet the embellishment and sew it securely onto the ear warmer.

BASIC BEANIE

This process creates a basic beanie with a smooth, even texture, perfect for chilly days. The simplicity of the design makes it a great project for beginners, offering a chance to practice and perfect the hdc stitch while creating a functional and stylish item.

DIFFICULTY LEVEL: Beginner

FINISHED MEASUREMENT: Approximately 7 inches in diameter and 9 inches in length (from the crown to the bottom edge) for a common adult size.

MATERIALS:

- Medium-weight yarn (worsted)
- Crochet hook size H/8 (5mm)
- Yarn needle
- Scissors

ABBREVIATIONS USED:

- ch: chain
- sl st: slip stitch
- hdc: half double crochet
- sc: single crochet

STEP-BY-STEP INSTRUCTIONS:

1. Begin by creating a slip knot to place on your crochet hook.

2. Ch 4 and join with a sl st to form a ring. This small ring will serve as the starting point for your beanie.

3. For the first round, ch 2 (this counts as your first hdc). Work 11 hdc into the center of the ring, then join with a sl st to the top of the initial chain 2. You should now have a total of 12 hdc. This forms the crown of the beanie.

4. Moving on to the second round, ch 2 (again, counting as the first hdc). Work 2 hdc in each stitch around, then join with a sl st to the top of the chain 2. You will have doubled the number of stitches to 24 hdc. This increases the diameter of the beanie crown.

5. For the third round, ch 2 and then work one hdc in the first stitch. In the next stitch, work 2 hdc. Continue this pattern around (one hdc in the next stitch, 2 hdc in the following stitch), and join with a sl st to the top of the chain 2. This alternating pattern increases the stitch count in a way that ensures the beanie expands evenly, creating a flat circle.

6. Continue increasing rounds in a similar manner, following the established pattern of increases. Each round will increase the number of stitches between the increases by one. For example, after a round of [one hdc, 2 hdc in the next], the next round will be [one hdc in the next two stitches, 2 hdc in the following stitch]. This method of gradual increases is crucial for shaping the dome of the beanie.

7. Keep working in rounds until the crown of the beanie reaches the desired diameter for the intended head size. A common measurement for an adult beanie is about 7 inches in diameter before stopping increases for a snug fit.

8. Once the crown has reached the desired size, stop increasing. Continue to crochet one hdc in each stitch around without increasing. This will start to form the sides of the beanie, creating the depth needed to cover the head.

CONTINUED →

9. As you work each round, the beanie will begin to curve inward, forming the classic beanie shape. Continue adding rounds until the beanie reaches the desired length. Typically, for an adult size, this will be about 7 to 9 inches from the crown to the bottom edge.

10. To finish, after completing the final round, cut the yarn, leaving a tail long enough to weave in with a yarn needle. Pull the tail through the last loop on your hook and tighten to secure. Weave in any loose ends for a neat finish.

For those looking to personalize their beanie further, consider adding a decorative edge or incorporating color changes.

TO ADD A RIBBED BRIM for texture and additional warmth, switch to a smaller hook, such as a size G/6 (4mm), after completing the body of the beanie.

1. Begin by chaining one and then work a round of sc around the bottom edge of the beanie.

2. In the next round, start creating the ribbed effect by working in the back loops only of each sc from the previous round.

3. Continue this pattern for about 3 to 5 rounds, or until the brim reaches your desired width. The ribbing will not only add an aesthetic touch but also provide a snugger fit around the head.

TO INTRODUCE COLOR CHANGES AND ADD STRIPES OR BLOCKS OF COLOR, simply cut the yarn at the end of a round, leaving a tail to weave in later. Join the new color yarn with a slip stitch and continue crocheting as before. When changing colors, ensure to weave in ends securely to prevent them from unraveling. This technique can be used to create a variety of patterns, from simple stripes to more complex designs, allowing for endless customization options.

FOR THOSE INTERESTED IN ADDING A POM-POM TO THE TOP OF THE BEANIE, there are several methods to create one. Using the same yarn as the beanie, wrap the yarn around your fingers or a piece of cardboard multiple times until you have a thick bundle. Tie a piece of yarn tightly around the middle of the bundle, then cut through the loops on either side and trim to form a pom-pom. Attach it securely to the top of the beanie by threading the ends of the tie through to the inside of the beanie and knotting them together.

Feel free to experiment with different embellishments to create beanies that reflect your personal style and creativity.

SHAWL

DIFFICULTY LEVEL: Beginner

FINAL MEASUREMENT: The finished shawl will measure approximately 60 inches wide by 30 inches long.

GAUGE: While gauge is not critical for a shawl, aiming for about 13 single crochets by 14 rows to make a 4x4 inch square can help ensure your shawl has a nice drape.

MATERIALS NEEDED:

- Medium-weight yarn (worsted) – approximately 400 grams. Opt for a soft acrylic or wool blend for warmth and ease of care.
- Crochet hook size H/8 (5mm)
- Scissors
- Yarn needle

ABBREVIATIONS USED:

- ch: chain
- sc: single crochet
- dc: double crochet
- sl st: slip stitch

STEP-BY-STEP INSTRUCTIONS:

1. Starting Your Shawl: Begin with a slip knot on your crochet hook, then ch 4. Join with a sl st to form a ring. This small ring will be the starting point of your shawl, from which you'll build outwards in triangular fashion.

2. Row 1: Ch 3 (this counts as your first dc), then work 3 dc into the center of the ring, ch 2, and work another 4 dc into the center of the ring. Turn your work. You have now started the increase pattern that will continue throughout your shawl.

3. Row 2: Ch 3 (first dc), work 2 dc in the first stitch, dc in each stitch to the center chain space. In the center chain space, work [2 dc, chain 2, 2 dc] to create the tip of the shawl. Continue with dc in each stitch to the last stitch, then work 3 dc in the last stitch. Turn your work.

4. Subsequent Rows: Repeat Row 2, maintaining the increase pattern at the beginning and end of each row, as well as at the center chain space. This increase pattern creates the triangular shape of the shawl. Continue until the shawl reaches your desired size, typically around 60 inches wide by 30 inches long.

5. Adding a Border (Optional): Once your shawl has reached the desired size, you may choose to add a simple border for a finished look. Simply sc around the entire edge of the shawl, working 3 sc in each corner to maintain the shape. For a more decorative edge, consider a picot or shell stitch border.

6. Finishing Touches: Cut the yarn, leaving a tail. Pull the tail through the last loop on your hook and tighten to secure. Weave in all ends with your yarn needle to ensure your shawl looks neat and tidy.

CONSIDERATIONS AND RECOMMENDATIONS:

- To ensure your shawl drapes beautifully, pay attention to the tension of your stitches. A looser tension is recommended for a softer drape, which is particularly desirable in a shawl. If you find your stitches are too tight, consider using a larger hook size to adjust.
- Upon completing the crochet portion of your shawl, take time to properly finish your work. Blocking your shawl can significantly improve its shape and drape. To block, soak your shawl in lukewarm water with a gentle wool wash, then carefully squeeze out excess water (avoid wringing). Pin the shawl into shape on a blocking mat, stretching it slightly to define the triangular shape and open up the stitches. Let it dry completely before removing the pins.

SCARF

Choose a color that suits your style or consider making the scarf as a gift and select a color that the recipient will love. For a longer scarf, you may need more than one skein of yarn, so plan accordingly based on the final length you desire.

DIFFICULTY LEVEL: Beginner

FINISHED MEASUREMENT: A standard scarf length is about 60 inches, but you can adjust this based on personal preference.

MATERIALS:

- Medium-weight yarn (worsted)
- Crochet hook size H/8 (5mm)
- Yarn needle
- Scissors

ABBREVIATIONS USED:

- ch: chain
- sl st: slip stitch
- sc: single crochet
- hdc: half double crochet

STEP-BY-STEP INSTRUCTIONS:

1. Starting Your Scarf: Begin by creating a slip knot.

2. Creating the Foundation Chain: Ch 30 for a standard-width scarf. This number can be adjusted to make the scarf wider or narrower based on personal preference.

3. First Row: For the first row, you will work in single crochet. Continue to sc in each chain across the row. At the end of the row, you should have 29 single crochets.

4. Creating the Body of the Scarf: Ch 1 and turn your work to start the next row. The chain 1 does not count as a stitch. Work a sc into the first stitch and each stitch across the row. At the end of each row, ch 1 and turn your work. Repeat this process to build the length of your scarf.

5. Measuring Your Work: As you crochet, periodically measure the length of your scarf. A standard scarf length is about 60 inches, but you can adjust this based on personal preference or the height of the person who will be wearing the scarf.

6. Checking Your Tension: It's important to maintain consistent tension as you crochet to ensure that your scarf is even in width and length. If you notice that your stitches are too tight or too loose, adjust your grip on the crochet hook or the way you are holding the yarn.

As you progress with your scarf, you may decide to add a bit of texture or visual interest to your creation. Introducing a new stitch, such as the half double crochet (hdc), can add a subtle ribbed effect that enhances the overall look and feel of the scarf.

TO INCORPORATE THE HDC STITCH, start at the beginning of a new row after completing your initial single crochet sections.

1. Yarn over before inserting your hook into the first stitch of the new row.

2. Insert the hook, yarn over again, and pull up a loop. You should now have three loops on your hook.

3. Yarn over once more and pull through all three loops on the hook. This completes one hdc.

4. Continue to hdc in each stitch across the row. At the end, ch 1 and turn your work to start the next row.

5. Alternate a few rows of sc with a few rows of hdc to create a textured pattern throughout the length of your scarf.

ADDING A BORDER:

Once you have reached the desired length for your scarf, finishing with a border can give it a polished look. A simple single crochet border works well for this project and can help to tidy up any uneven edges.

1. Start your border by attaching the yarn with a sl st to any corner of the scarf.

2. Ch 1, then work a sc evenly around the entire perimeter of the scarf, placing 3 sc in each corner to maintain a flat edge.

3. Join with a sl st to the first sc of the border, then cut your yarn and weave in the ends with your yarn needle.

4. Finishing Touches: To finish your scarf, use your yarn needle to weave in any remaining loose ends. This will help to secure your work and ensure that the scarf holds up well with wear and washing.

If desired, **YOU CAN ALSO ADD FRINGE** to the ends of your scarf to give it an extra decorative touch.

1. Cut several lengths of yarn twice as long as you want the fringe to be.

2. Fold these pieces in half, then use your crochet hook to pull the looped end through the edge of the scarf and thread the cut ends through the loop. Pull tight to secure.

3. Repeat this process along the short ends of the scarf, spacing the fringe evenly.

CARE INSTRUCTIONS:

To keep your scarf at its best, follow the care instructions on the yarn label. Most medium-weight yarns are machine washable, but hand washing and laying flat to dry can help to preserve the texture and shape of your crochet work.

BLANKET

DIFFICULTY LEVEL: Intermediate

FINISHED MEASUREMENT: Approximately 50 inches by 60 inches, a standard size for a throw blanket.

GAUGE: Gauge of 13 single crochets by 14 rows equals 4 inches square.

MATERIALS:

- Medium-weight yarn (worsted)
- Crochet hook size H/8 (5mm)
- Yarn needle
- Scissors

ABBREVIATIONS USED:

- ch: chain
- sl st: slip stitch
- sc: single crochet
- hdc: half double crochet
- dc: double crochet

STEP-BY-STEP INSTRUCTIONS:

1. Begin by making a slip knot on your crochet hook.

2. Ch 150 stitches. This will form the width of your blanket. Keep the stitches loose enough for flexibility but tight enough to maintain an even texture.

3. Make a sc. Continue with sc in every chain across the row. You will have 149 sc.

4. Turning Your Work: At the end of the first row, chain one (this counts as the first stitch of the next row), then turn your work to start the next row.

5. Building Rows: Start the second row by inserting the hook into the first stitch, making a sc and continue single crocheting across the row. Repeat this process for each row. To create a textured look, you can alternate between different stitches, such as the hdc or dc, every few rows.

6. Changing Colors (Optional): To add interest to your blanket, you may wish to change colors. To do this, cut the yarn, leaving a six-inch tail. Join the new color yarn with a sl st in the last stitch of the old color. Continue crocheting as before with the new color.

7. Cut the yarn, leaving a six-inch tail. Yarn over and pull the tail through the loop on your hook to secure it. Weave in all ends with a yarn needle to give your blanket a neat appearance. This step is crucial for ensuring your blanket doesn't unravel and looks tidy and professional.

TO ADD A BORDER TO YOUR BLANKET:

1. Select a contrasting or complementary color and attach the yarn to any corner of the blanket using a sl st.

2. You can then crochet around the perimeter of the blanket, using sc, hdc, or even a simple picot edge for a delicate finish. Remember to make three stitches in each corner to maintain a flat edge.

CONSIDERATIONS AND RECOMMENDATIONS:

- As you progress, remember to count your stitches periodically to ensure that the blanket's width remains consistent. If you find that your edges are becoming uneven, you may need to adjust your tension or count your stitches more frequently to correct the issue.

- To ensure your blanket grows evenly, it's important to check your gauge every few rows. If you notice your stitches are too tight or too loose compared to the gauge, adjust your tension accordingly. This might mean crocheting a bit looser or tighter, or even switching to a different hook size if necessary. Consistency is key to achieving a professional-looking finish.

- Caring for your blanket is straightforward. Most medium-weight yarns are machine washable, but always check the yarn label for specific care instructions. Washing your blanket in cool water and tumble drying on low will keep it looking fresh and cozy for years to come.

PILLOW

DIFFICULTY LEVEL: Intermediate

FINISHED MEASUREMENT: The finished pillow cover will measure approximately 16x16 inches, a common size that fits standard pillow inserts.

COLORS: Select two colors that complement your decor. For a subtle look, choose colors within the same palette. For something more striking, opt for contrasting colors.

GAUGE: Gauge is not crucial for this project, but for best results, aim for a gauge of approximately 13 single crochets by 14 rows to make a 4x4 inch square. Adjust your hook size if necessary to achieve this gauge.

MATERIALS NEEDED:

- Medium-weight yarn (worsted) in two colors of your choice. Consider a soft acrylic or cotton blend for durability and ease of care.
- Crochet hook size H/8 (5mm)
- Scissors
- Yarn needle
- Pillow insert or stuffing material, depending on whether you're making a pillow cover or a stuffed pillow.

ABBREVIATIONS USED:

- ch: chain
- sc: single crochet
- dc: double crochet
- sl st: slip stitch

STEP-BY-STEP INSTRUCTIONS:

1. Starting Your Pillow Cover: Begin by creating a slip knot and ch 61. This initial chain will form the width of your pillow cover. Ensure that your chain is not too tight to maintain even tension throughout your work.

2. Creating the First Row: For the first row, insert your hook into the second chain from the hook and work a sc. Continue to sc in each chain across the row. You will have 60 sc at the end of this row. Ch 1 and turn your work.

3. Building the Body of the Pillow Cover: Continue working in sc, chaining 1 and turning at the end of each row. To introduce a second color, finish the last stitch of your current color by pulling through the new color in the final yarn over. Cut the old color, leaving a tail to weave in later, and continue with the new color. Alternate colors as desired to create stripes or blocks of color.

4. Creating Texture (Optional): To add texture to your pillow cover, you can incorporate simple stitch variations. For example, every few rows, work a row of dc instead of sc. To do this, ch 3 at the beginning of the row (counts as the first dc), then yarn over, insert the hook into the next stitch, yarn over and pull up a loop, yarn over and pull through two loops, yarn over again and pull through the remaining two loops on the hook.

5. Finishing the Front Panel: Continue crocheting until the piece measures approximately 16 inches from the starting chain, ending with a final row of sc for a neat edge. Fasten off and weave in any loose ends with your yarn needle.

6. To create the back panel of your pillow cover, follow the same steps as the front panel until you reach the desired length, typically matching the front at approximately 16 inches. If you're aiming for a pillow cover with a closure, consider stopping about an inch shorter on the back panel to accommodate for the overlap or closure mechanism.

CREATING A CLOSURE:

For a simple yet effective closure, you can opt for button loops or ties. Here's how to add button loops:

1. Button Loops:
- At the end of your back panel, instead of fastening off, ch a length that can loop over a button comfortably, usually about 3-5 ch, depending on the size of your buttons.
- Skip 2-3 stitches, then secure the loop with a sl st into the next stitch.
- Repeat this process across the top of the back panel, ensuring you have an even number of loops for your buttons. Space the loops evenly, aiming for about 4-6 loops depending on the width of your panel.

2. Sewing on Buttons:
- Lay the front and back panels together, with the wrong sides facing each other, aligning the edges.
- Position your buttons on the front panel, directly opposite the loops on the back panel. Sew them in place securely, making sure they align with the loops for easy closure.

JOINING THE PANELS:

With both panels completed and the closure prepared, it's time to join them together:

1. Align the Panels:
- Place the panels with the right sides facing each other, ensuring the edges match up.
- If you've created a flap for the closure, place the back panel on top of the front panel, aligning the bottom edges.

2. Seaming:
- Using a length of yarn and your yarn needle, begin seaming the panels together with a sl st for a crochet join. Start from one corner and work your way around three sides of the pillow, leaving the side with the closure open.
- Be sure to work the stitches evenly and not too tightly, to maintain a consistent edge.

3. Adding the Pillow Insert:
- Once three sides are joined, turn the pillow cover right side out through the open side.
- Insert your pillow form or stuffing material into the cover, adjusting it to fit snugly and evenly within the cover.

4. Closing the Pillow Cover:
- Align the open edges of the pillow cover, and using the same method as the other three sides, seam the final side closed.
- If you've added a flap for the closure, simply button up the loops to secure the back panel over the front.

FINISHING TOUCHES:

After your pillow is fully assembled, give it a final inspection for any loose ends that may need weaving in or buttons that require additional securing. Fluff up the pillow insert to ensure the cover is fully filled out and presents a plump, inviting appearance.

BAG

DIFFICULTY LEVEL: Intermediate

FINISHED MEASUREMENT: The finished bag will measure approximately 12 inches wide by 10 inches high, not including the handles.

GAUGE: Gauge is important to ensure your bag comes out the right size and uses the amount of yarn specified. For this project, a gauge of 13 single crochets by 14 rows equals a 4x4 inch square. If your gauge is off, adjust your hook size accordingly.

MATERIALS NEEDED:

- Medium-weight yarn (worsted) in your choice of color. Consider using about 300 grams of yarn for a bag that's both durable and lightweight. Opt for a cotton or a cotton-blend yarn for durability and ease of care. Cotton yarn holds its shape well and is strong enough to carry weight, making it an ideal choice for a tote bag.
- Crochet hook size H/8 (5mm)
- Scissors
- Yarn needle

ABBREVIATIONS USED:

- ch: chain
- sc: single crochet
- sl st: slip stitch

STEP-BY-STEP INSTRUCTIONS:

1. Creating the Base of the Bag: Begin by making a slip knot on your crochet hook, then ch 46. This chain forms the foundation of your bag's base. Ensure the chain is not too tight to allow for even stitches in the next row.

2. Forming the First Row: Insert your hook into the second chain from the hook, then work a sc. Continue to sc in each chain across. At the end of the row, you will have 45 sc. Ch 1 and turn your work to start the next row.

3. Building the Body of the Bag: Continue working in sc, chaining 1 at the beginning of each row. This creates a sturdy fabric for the bag. After completing a few rows, you can check your gauge to ensure the bag will be the correct size. Continue crocheting in rows until the piece measures approximately 10 inches from the starting chain.

4. Creating the Sides and Bottom of the Bag: Once the base piece measures 10 inches in height, do not cut the yarn. Instead, pivot your work to crochet along the side of the base. Work evenly spaced sc along the side, approximately 30 sc. When you reach the corner, ch 1 to turn the corner, then continue along the bottom edge of the base, working 1 sc into each chain of the starting chain. Repeat this process along the other side and top edge to create a border that adds structure to the bag.

5. Forming the Bag's Body: After completing the border around the base, continue to work in rounds to build the sides of the bag. Do not join at the end of each round; instead, work in a spiral to avoid creating a seam. Use a stitch marker to mark the beginning of each round. Continue working in sc until the bag's body measures about 10 inches tall from the base.

To finish the body of your crochet bag and add handles for easy carrying, follow these detailed steps:

6. Completing the Body: Once the bag's body reaches approximately 10 inches in height, it's time to create a finishing edge to give it a polished look. Work a sc in each stitch around the top of the bag. Then, to create a more defined edge, you can do a round of sl st in each sc from the previous round. This not only adds strength to the top edge but also provides a neater finish.

7. Creating the Handles: For the handles, decide on the length you prefer, but a standard is about 20 inches for a comfortable shoulder strap.
- To start a handle, ch 1 at any point along the bag's top edge.
- Then, sc 5 stitches spaced evenly apart.
- Ch 70 (or more for a longer handle), skip the next 20 stitches on the bag's top edge (adjust this number based on the bag's width and your preferred handle width), and attach the chain to the bag with a sc in the next stitch.
- Work 4 more sc spaced evenly (total of 5 sc on the other side of the handle base). This creates one handle.
- To reinforce the handle, work back along the chain with sc and join with a sl st to the starting point of the handle on the bag's edge. Repeat this process on the opposite side of the bag for the second handle.

8. Reinforcing the Handles: For added durability, work another row of sc along both sides of each handle. This not only strengthens the handle but also makes it more comfortable to hold. Once you reach the base of the handle where it attaches to the bag, work a sl st around the sc posts from the previous round to anchor the handle securely.

9. Finishing Touches: To complete your bag, cut the yarn, leaving a tail long enough to weave in with a yarn needle. Carefully weave in all ends to secure them and prevent unraveling. For a cleaner look, weave the ends through the stitches of the same color.

10. Optional Decorative Elements: Personalize your bag by adding decorative elements such as crochet flowers, appliques, or buttons. These can be attached to the bag's body or along the edge of the handles for a unique touch. To attach, use a yarn needle and the same yarn used for the bag, sewing each element securely in place.

11. Blocking Your Bag: For a professional finish, consider blocking your bag. This process involves wetting or steaming the bag to set the shape and size. Lay the bag flat on a towel and gently shape it to the desired dimensions. Allow it to dry completely before using. Blocking is especially helpful if your bag came out a bit uneven or if you want to ensure it hangs nicely when carried.

GLOVES

DIFFICULTY LEVEL: Intermediate

FINISHED MEASUREMENT: The finished gloves should fit an average adult hand. However, adjustments can be made for a custom fit by altering the number of starting chains or rows.

GAUGE: Gauge is crucial for ensuring your gloves fit well. Aim for a gauge of 16 single crochets by 20 rows to make a 4x4 inch square. Adjust your hook size if necessary to achieve this gauge.

MATERIALS NEEDED:

- Medium-weight yarn (worsted) in your color of choice. For a pair of gloves, approximately 100 grams should suffice. Choose a yarn that is soft yet durable. Acrylic, wool, or a blend are ideal choices for gloves as they offer warmth and comfort against the skin.
- Crochet hook size H/8 (5mm)
- Scissors
- Yarn needle

ABBREVIATIONS USED:

- ch: chain
- sl st: slip stitch
- sc: single crochet
- hdc: half double crochet

STEP-BY-STEP INSTRUCTIONS:

1. Starting the Cuff: Begin by making a slip knot on your crochet hook, then ch 30. This chain forms the foundation of your glove's cuff. Join with a sl st to form a ring, ensuring not to twist the chain.

2. Cuff Ribbing: Ch 2 (this counts as your first hdc). Work a hdc in the back loop only of each chain around. Join with a sl st to the top of the initial ch 2. This creates a ribbed effect for the cuff. Repeat this process for approximately 10 rows, or until the cuff reaches your desired length.

3. Creating the Hand: After completing the cuff, do not cut the yarn. Instead, pivot your work to crochet along the edge of the cuff. Evenly space 36 sc around the edge of the cuff. This transition from the cuff to the hand creates the base for the glove's body.

4. Increasing for Thumb Gusset: Continue working in the round, single crocheting in each stitch. To form the thumb gusset, you'll need to increase stitches in a specific area. In the next round, place a marker in the 18th stitch. Make 2 sc in this marked stitch and in each of the next 2 stitches. In the following rounds, increase by making 2 sc in the stitch before and after the previous round's increases until you have a total of 12 stitches in the thumb gusset area.

5. Separating the Thumb: Once the thumb gusset has reached 12 stitches, sl st in the next stitch to round off the gusset. Cut the yarn, leaving a long tail, and pull through the last loop to secure. You will later reattach the yarn to continue working the body of the glove.

This initial part of the glove-making process introduces you to the foundational steps of crafting a pair of crochet gloves, including creating a ribbed cuff, forming the hand, and increasing for the thumb gusset. With these basics established, you're well on your way to completing your very own handmade gloves.

To proceed with the glove, reattach the yarn at the base of the thumb gusset, ensuring to leave a tail for weaving in later.

6. Begin by inserting your hook into the first stitch after the gusset and pull through the yarn. Ch 1 to secure and start sc around the hand's body, skipping over the thumb gusset stitches. This creates the separation between the thumb and the rest of the fingers. Continue sc in each stitch around until the glove's body, from the cuff to the top, measures about 6 inches or reaches the base of the fingers.

7. For the finger divisions, you will work individual sections for each finger, starting with the pinky. To create the pinky, identify and mark the last 8 stitches on one side of the glove. Join the yarn with a sl st near the first marked stitch, ch 1, and sc in the same stitch and in each of the next 7 stitches around the marked area. Work in rounds until the pinky section measures about 2.5 inches or covers the pinky finger. Finish off by slip stitching the last round and cutting the yarn, leaving a tail for weaving in.

8. Next, move to the ring finger, attaching the yarn with a sl st to the base where the pinky finger starts. Ch 1, then sc in the same space, picking up stitches around the hand and using a similar number of stitches as for the pinky, usually around 8 to 10 stitches. Work in rounds until this section also measures about 2.5 inches or covers the ring finger.

9. Repeat the process for the middle and index fingers, adjusting the number of stitches as needed to accommodate the larger size of these fingers, typically 10 to 12 stitches for the middle finger and 8 to 10 stitches for the index finger.

10. For the thumb, reattach the yarn at the base of the thumb gusset with a slip stitch. Ch 1, then sc around the gusset opening, distributing stitches evenly to cover the thumb, usually requiring 12 to 14 stitches. Work in rounds until the thumb section covers the entire thumb, approximately 2 inches.

11. Once all fingers and the thumb are completed, use the yarn needle to weave in all ends securely. For a finished look, you may choose to work a single crochet edge around the finger openings if desired, although this is optional.

To ensure both gloves are symmetrical, repeat the same process for the second glove, mirroring the increases for the thumb gusset and the placement of the fingers. Pay close attention to the gauge and stitch count to ensure both gloves match in size and fit.

SIMPLE CARDIGAN

DIFFICULTY LEVEL: Intermediate

FINISHED MEASUREMENT: Aim for a finished bust measurement of around 36-38 inches for a medium size. Adjust the number of starting chains if a larger or smaller size is desired.

GAUGE: Gauge is important to ensure your cardigan fits well. Aim for a gauge of 16 stitches and 22 rows = 4x4 inches in single crochet (sc).

MATERIALS NEEDED:

- Medium-weight yarn (worsted) – Approximately 1000-1200 yards, depending on the size of the cardigan. Choose a soft, comfortable yarn that's easy to work with. Acrylic, cotton, or a blend are excellent choices.
- Crochet hook size H/8 (5mm)
- Scissors
- Yarn needle
- Stitch markers
- Measuring tape

ABBREVIATIONS USED:

- ch: chain
- sl st: slip stitch
- sc: single crochet
- hdc: half double crochet

STEP-BY-STEP INSTRUCTIONS:

1. Starting the Back Panel: Begin by ch 74 (for a medium size). This will form the foundation of the cardigan's back panel. Ensure your chain is not too tight to allow for flexibility and comfort in the finished piece.

2. First Row: Starting from the second chain from the hook, work a sc into each chain across. You will have 73 sc. Ch 1 and turn your work. This chain 1 does not count as a stitch.

3. Building the Back Panel: Continue working in sc back and forth across each row. To create a textured look, you can alternate between sc and hdc rows. For instance, after a row of sc, work a row of hdc by chaining 2 (counts as the first hdc), then hdc in each stitch across. Alternate these two rows to build the back panel. Continue until the panel measures approximately 22 inches in length, or desired length to the underarm.

4. Shaping the Armholes: Once the back panel reaches the desired length, it's time to shape the armholes. To do this, decrease at the beginning and end of the next two rows. For a simple decrease, work the first two stitches together, then continue in pattern until the last two stitches, and work these two together as well.

5. Continuing the Body: After shaping the armholes, continue working in your established pattern (alternating between sc and hdc rows) until the back panel measures approximately 30 inches in total length, or your desired length from the shoulder to the bottom edge of the cardigan.

This forms the foundational back piece of your simple cardigan. The next steps will involve creating the front panels and sleeves, joining the pieces, and adding finishing touches to complete your garment.

For the front panels, you will create two separate pieces that mirror each other.

FRONT PANELS:

1. Starting the First Front Panel: Ch 38 for a medium size, aiming for a width that's about half of the back panel, adjusting the number of chains for size as needed. Work in the same pattern as the back panel, starting with a row of sc from the second chain from the hook and alternating with hdc rows for texture.

2. Building the Front Panel: Continue in the established pattern until this piece matches the length of the back panel up to the armhole shaping, approximately 22 inches.

3. Shaping the Armhole: Just like the back panel, decrease at the beginning and end of the next two rows to shape the armhole. Then, continue in pattern until the front panel measures the same length as the back panel, approximately 30 inches.

4. Creating the Neckline: When the front panel matches the back panel in length, begin to shape the neckline. To do this, continue in your established pattern but decrease at the neck edge every other row. For a simple decrease, work the first two stitches together at the neck edge, then continue in pattern across. Repeat these decreases until about half of the stitches remain, then continue straight until the piece measures the same length as the back panel. Repeat these steps for the second front panel, mirroring the decreases to ensure the neckline shapes correctly.

SLEEVES:

1. Starting the Sleeve: Chain 50 (adjust the number of chains for size as needed), ensuring the chain is not too tight. This will form the cuff of the sleeve. Work in sc from the second chain from the hook for the first row, then continue in established pattern, alternating between sc and hdc rows.

2. Increasing for Sleeve Width: To shape the sleeve, increase at both ends of every 6th row. To increase, work two stitches into the same stitch at both the beginning and end of these rows. Continue these increases until the sleeve measures approximately 18 inches in width at the widest part.

3. Shaping the Cap of the Sleeve: Once the sleeve reaches the desired width, begin to decrease at both ends of every other row to shape the cap of the sleeve. Continue these decreases until the sleeve cap fits the armhole opening, approximately 20 rows.

JOINING THE PIECES:

1. Shoulder Seams: Lay the back panel flat and place the front panels on top, right sides facing together. Align the shoulder edges and use stitch markers to hold the pieces in place. Seam the shoulders together using a yarn needle and matching yarn.

2. Attaching the Sleeves: Align the center of each sleeve with the shoulder seam and use stitch markers to secure the sleeves in place. Seam around the armhole, attaching the sleeve to the body of the cardigan.

3. Side and Sleeve Seams: Fold the cardigan with right sides together, aligning the front and back panels and the edges of the sleeves. Seam from the bottom edge of the cardigan up the side and continue along the underside of the sleeve in one continuous seam. Repeat on the other side.

FINISHING TOUCHES:

1. Edging: For a clean finish, work a sc edge around the entire cardigan, including the front panels, bottom edge, and neckline. This not only defines the edges but also helps to prevent stretching.

2. Fastenings: If desired, add buttons or toggles to the front panels. Sew buttonholes on one side and attach the toggles or buttons opposite them, ensuring they line up correctly.

3. Weaving in Ends: Use a yarn needle to weave in any remaining loose ends for a neat finish.

EASY CHRISTMAS PROJECTS

Now, for the special Christmas festivities, here are a few simple projects to get you started:

CHRISTMAS TREE ORNAMENT

DIFFICULTY LEVEL: Beginner

FINISHED MEASUREMENT: Approximately 5 inches tall including the star

GAUGE: Not critical for this project, but if your stitches are very loose, consider using a smaller hook to prevent the stuffing from showing.

MATERIALS:

- Green worsted weight yarn (Category 4)
- Small amount of brown and yellow worsted weight yarn (Category 4) for decorations
- Size G-6 (4mm) crochet hook
- Scissors
- Tapestry needle
- Polyester fiberfill for stuffing
- Optional: Small jingle bells or beads for decoration

COLORS:

- Main color: Green for the tree
- Additional colors: Brown for the trunk, Yellow for the star

ABBREVIATIONS USED:

- ch = chain
- sc = single crochet
- dc = double crochet
- sl st = slip stitch
- st(s) = stitch(es)

STEP-BY-STEP INSTRUCTIONS:

1. Tree Body:
- Start with green yarn.
- Make a magic ring.
- Round 1: Ch 2 (counts as first dc), 9 dc in ring, sl st to first dc to join (10 dc).
- Round 2: Ch 2, dc in same st as joining, 2 dc in each st around, sl st to first dc to join (20 dc).
- Round 3-5: Repeat Round 2, increasing 10 dc in each round (50 dc in Round 5).
- Fasten off after Round 5.

2. Tree Trunk:
- Switch to brown yarn.
- Pick up a stitch at the bottom center of the tree body.
- Ch 1, work 6 sc evenly around to form a circle, sl st to first sc to join.
- Rounds 1-3: Ch 1, sc in each st around, sl st to first sc to join (6 sc).
- Fasten off after Round 3.

3. Star (Top Decoration):
- Switch to yellow yarn.
- Ch 3, sl st in first ch to form a ring.
- * Ch 3, sl st in ring repeat from * to 4 more times (5 points).
- Fasten off, leaving a long tail for attaching to the top of the tree.

4. Assembly:
- Stuff the tree body with polyester fiberfill to the desired consistency.
- Using the tapestry needle, sew the star to the top of the tree.
- Optional: Sew small jingle bells or beads onto the tree as decorations.

5. Finishing:
- Weave in all ends securely.
- Optional: Create a loop with a piece of yarn and attach it to the top of the tree if you wish to hang it as an ornament.

CHRISTMAS STOCKING

DIFFICULTY LEVEL: Beginner

FINISHED MEASUREMENT: The stocking will measure approximately 18 inches in length from top to toe and 7 inches in width at the widest part of the foot.

COLORS: Traditional Christmas colors: red for the body, white for the cuff, and green for decorative detailing.

GAUGE:

- 13 single crochet stitches = 4 inches
- 14 rows = 4 inches

MATERIALS:

- Red, white, and green worsted weight yarn (Category 4)
- Size H-8 (5mm) crochet hook
- Scissors
- Tapestry needle
- Stitch markers

ABBREVIATIONS USED:

- ch = chain
- sc = single crochet
- hdc = half double crochet
- sl st = slip stitch
- st(s) = stitch(es)
- sc2tog = single crochet decrease

STEP-BY-STEP INSTRUCTIONS:

1. Start with the Cuff:
- Using white yarn, ch 14.
- Row 1: sc in the 2nd ch from the hook and in each ch across, turn. (13 sc)
- Rows 2-40: ch 1, working in the back loops only, sc in each sc across, turn.
- After completing Row 40, do not cut the yarn. Fold the cuff piece in half with the short ends together, and sl st through both layers to join into a cuff. Do not turn.

2. Transition to the Stocking Body:
- Change to red yarn.
- Round 1: Work 40 sc evenly spaced around the top edge of the cuff. Join with a sl st to the first sc.
- Round 2-50: ch 1, sc in each sc around, join with a sl st to the first sc.
- Begin to decrease for the heel after Round 50 as follows:
- Row 1 (Heel): Ch 1, sc in the next 10 sts, turn.
- Row 2: Skip the first st, sc in the next 8 sts, skip the next st, sc in the last st, turn.
- Repeat Row 2, decreasing by 2 sts each row until 2 sts remain. Sl st the 2 remaining sts together.

3. Form the Foot:
- Pick up and sc around the heel opening, then continue working in rounds down the length of the foot.
- Round 1-20: Ch 1, sc in each sc around, join with a sl st to the first sc.
- Start decreasing for the toe in Round 21 as follows:
- Round 21: * Sc in the next 2 sts, sc2tog; repeat from * around, join with a sl st to the first sc.
- Repeat this decrease pattern every round until 8 sts remain.
- Final Round: Sc2tog 4 times. Fasten off, leaving a long tail. Use the tail to sew the toe closed.

4. Add Decorative Details:
- Using green yarn, embroider small holly leaves or other Christmas motifs onto the stocking.
- Create a hanging loop: With red yarn, ch 20, sl st to form a loop. Fasten off. Sew the loop to the inside top corner of the stocking.

5. Finishing:
- Weave in all ends using a tapestry needle.
- Optionally, add a pompom or other decorations to the cuff for extra festivity.

CHRISTMAS WREATH

DIFFICULTY LEVEL: Beginner to Intermediate

FINISHED MEASUREMENT: The completed wreath will measure approximately 14 inches in diameter, fitting perfectly on most doors

COLORS:

- Primary color: Green for the wreath
- Decoration colors: Red, white, and gold for a festive look

GAUGE: Not critical for this project, but aim for a firm fabric that holds its shape

MATERIALS:

- Green worsted weight yarn (Category 4) for the wreath base
- Assorted colors of worsted weight yarn (Category 4) for decorations (red, white, gold)
- Size I-9 (5.5 mm) crochet hook
- Scissors
- Tapestry needle
- Wire wreath frame, 14 inches in diameter
- Floral wire

ABBREVIATIONS USED:

- ch = chain
- sc = single crochet
- dc = double crochet
- sl st = slip stitch

STEP-BY-STEP INSTRUCTIONS:

1. Creating the Wreath Base:
- Start by making a slip knot and chaining enough stitches to wrap around the wire wreath frame comfortably, approximately 150 chains, depending on your tension.
- Join with a sl st to form a circle, being careful not to twist the chain.
- Work in rounds of sc until the band covers the frame completely, usually about 6-8 rows.
- Fasten off and use a tapestry needle to weave in the ends securely.

2. Attaching the Base to the Frame:
- Lay your crocheted band over the wire wreath frame.
- Use floral wire to attach the crochet band to the frame at several points securely, ensuring it's evenly stretched around the frame.

3. Making the Decorations:
- Crochet small holly leaves by chaining 8, then working a series of dc, hdc, sc, and sl st along the chain for the leaf shape. Make 12-15 leaves.
- For berries, use red yarn to make small balls by working 6 sc into a magic ring, then increasing and decreasing to form a ball. Make 9-12 berries.
- Crochet bows or ribbons in gold yarn by creating a rectangular piece with chain stitches and double crochet, then wrapping the center tightly to form a bow shape. Make 2-3 bows.

4. Assembling the Wreath:
- Sew or use floral wire to attach the holly leaves in groups of three around the wreath at equal intervals.
- Attach the berries in clusters near the holly leaves with the tapestry needle and yarn or floral wire.
- Position the bows or ribbons on the wreath, securing them with floral wire or by sewing them on.

5. **Finishing Touches:**
- Use the tapestry needle to tuck in any loose ends from the decorations.
- Create a loop with green yarn at the top of the wreath to hang it.
- Adjust the decorations as needed to ensure a balanced, festive look.

CHAPTER 9
COMMON CROCHET PROBLEMS AND SOLUTIONS

1. LOOPS TOO TIGHT OR TOO LOOSE: Achieving even tension in crochet is crucial for the uniformity of your project. If your loops are too tight, you might struggle to insert your hook into them for the next stitch. Conversely, if they're too loose, your work may look sloppy and have inconsistent gaps.

To solve this, practice holding your yarn and hook in a way that feels comfortable yet gives you control over the yarn tension. A common method is to wrap the yarn around your pinky finger and then over your index finger, adjusting the wrap to increase or decrease tension.

2. STITCHES NOT LOOKING LIKE THE PATTERN: If your stitches don't resemble those in the pattern, first ensure you're using the correct stitch and check your gauge. The gauge determines how many stitches and rows per inch you should have.

If your gauge is off, adjust your hook size accordingly. Also, review the instructions to ensure you're executing the stitch correctly. Sometimes, watching a tutorial on the specific stitch can provide clarity.

3. JOINING NEW YARN LOOKS MESSY: When you need to add a new ball of yarn or change colors, it can sometimes result in a jarring transition or loose ends that are hard to hide.

To make the transition smoother, try joining the new yarn at the end of a row. Leave a tail of about 6 inches for both the old and new yarn, and crochet over these tails as you work the next few stitches. This can help secure the yarn and make the join less noticeable.

4. EDGES ARE UNEVEN: If the edges of your work are wavy or irregular, it might be because you're adding or missing stitches at the beginning or end of rows.

Make sure you're counting your stitches in each row and that you understand where the first and last stitch of each row should be placed. Placing a stitch marker in the first and last stitch of each row can help you keep track.

5. CROCHET FABRIC IS CURLING: Curling can occur if your stitches are too tight or if there's a significant difference in stitch height (such as mixing single crochet with taller stitches without proper adjustments).

To prevent curling, work on keeping an even tension and choose a hook size that matches the yarn weight and stitch pattern. Blocking your finished piece can also help to relax the stitches and reduce curling.

6. DIFFICULTY WORKING IN THE ROUND: Working in the round is common for many projects but can be tricky due to joining rounds and maintaining the correct stitch count.

Use a stitch marker to mark the beginning of each round to keep your place. If you're having trouble seeing the stitches, try using a lighter-colored yarn until you're more comfortable with the technique. Remember to count your stitches regularly to ensure you're not adding or missing any.

7. YARN SPLITTING: Using a hook that's too small or sharp can cause the yarn to split, making your work look messy and making it difficult to crochet.

Opt for hooks with a smooth finish and a rounded tip. Additionally, choose quality yarn that's tightly spun to minimize splitting. If you continue to struggle, consider changing your yarn brand or type for a better experience.

APPENDIX
GLOSSARY OF CROCHET TERMS AND ABBREVIATIONS

Back Loop (blo): It's the back of the horizontal bar. When indicated, only the back loop should be worked, leaving the front one unworked.

Chain (ch): A foundation technique where yarn is looped to form a series of chain stitches, starting with a slip knot.

Crochet Hook: A tool used to make crochet stitches, available in different sizes and materials.

Decrease (dec): Combining two or more stitches into one to narrow the fabric. Often used in shaping items like hats or amigurumi.

Double Crochet (dc): A fundamental crochet stitch that's twice the height of a single crochet.

Double Treble Crochet (dtr): One stitch higher than the double crochet, made by wrapping the yarn around the hook three times before inserting it into the stitch.

Extended Single Crochet (esc): A variant of the single crochet with an additional chain.

Fasten Off: The process of cutting the yarn and pulling the tail through the last loop on the hook to secure the work and prevent unraveling.

Foundation Chain: The initial chain that serves as the foundation for the rest of the project.

Front Loop (flo): It's the front of the horizontal bar. When indicated, only the front loop should be worked, leaving the back one unworked.

Gauge: The number of stitches and rows per centimeter or inch in the fabric.

Half Double Crochet (hdc): A stitch higher than a single crochet but shorter than a double crochet.

Increase (inc): Adding stitches to a row or round to widen the fabric. Typically involves making two stitches into the same stitch from the previous row or round.

Join Yarn: Join a new strand of yarn or close a row.

Loop: A loop of yarn on the hook.

Magic Ring (mr): A method of starting circular projects without leaving a hole in the center.

Picot Stitch: A small decorative chain stitch.

Popcorn Stitch: A group of stitches worked together and joined at the top.

Puff Stitch: A stitch that groups several loops and joins them at the top.

Repeat (rep): To make a series of stitches again.

Reverse Single Crochet: A single crochet in the opposite direction.

Right Side (RS): The side of the fabric that is usually shown.

Round (rnd): A complete lap in a circular project.

Row: A sequence of stitches in a linear project.

Shell Stitch: A group of double crochet stitches worked in the same stitch to form a shell.

Single Crochet (sc): A basic crochet stitch creating a tight, dense fabric.

Skip (sk): Omit one or more stitches.

Slip Knot: An adjustable knot used to start most crochet projects.

Slip Stitch (sl st): A method to join stitches with minimal height, moving yarn through both the stitch on the hook and the next stitch without yarning over.

Stitch Marker: A tool used for marking the beginning of a round or noting where increases or decreases occur.

Tail End: The loose end of the yarn that remains after starting or ending a project.

Treble Crochet (tr): A tall stitch three times the height of a single crochet.

Turn: Rotate the work to start a new row.

Turning Chain: The chain made at the end of a row to reach the necessary height for the next row.

V-Stitch: A special stitch that creates a pattern resembling the letter "V" by combining a series of double crochets and chain spaces.

Working End: The end of the yarn attached to the ball and is used for crocheting.

Wrong Side (WS): The side of the fabric that is not usually shown.

Yarn Over (YO): The action of wrapping the yarn over the crochet hook to create stitches, increases, or to secure a stitch at the end of a project.

HERE ARE YOUR BONUS VIDEOS!

Embark on your crochet journey with an invaluable resource right at your fingertips. See exactly how each stitch is executed with close-up views and detailed explanations.

STEP-BY-STEP GUIDANCE: Follow along with our video tutorials that take you through each crochet stitch and basic technique shown in the book. Perfect for beginners, these videos will help you master the basics with ease and confidence.

Unlock the Art of Crochet with Our Exclusive Bonus Videos!

SCAN HERE TO VIEW THEM

Made in the USA
Columbia, SC
06 January 2025